IELTS on Track

TEST PRACTICE Academic

• Stephen Slater • Donna Millen • Pat Tyrie

D1439503

Language Australia

Centre for English Language in the University of South Australia

I

Published by Language Australia Ltd.
in association with
The Centre for English Language
in the University of South Australia

Language Australia Ltd.
GPO Box 372 F
Melbourne, Victoria 3001
www.languageaustralia.com.au

First published January 2003

ISBN   1 876768 36 3   Book
ISBN   1 876768 38 X   (CD 1)
ISBN   1 876768 39 8   (CD 2)

CD duplication by Adelaide Tape Distributors
Cover and CD design by Doreen Inhofer

Printed by Hyde Park Press, 4 Deacon Avenue,
Richmond, South Australia 5033

THANKS & ACKNOWLEDGEMENTS

The authors and publisher would like to thank all the teachers and international students based in Australia, UK, Ukraine, and Japan for the valuable feedback during the trialling of these materials, particularly Anthony Hemmens, Deborah Newstead, Shaun Tiddy, Jacquie Moller, Cynthia Mchawala, and Dilwyn Jaye. Thanks also to Kaoru Nagata, Sonia Chhabra, Bruce Millen and Carsten Jensen for assistance with the development of speaking and listening material.

The authors gratefully acknowledge Zsuzso Molnar and Wen Lo for their participation in the sample speaking tests; Andrew Ellis, Rosemary Pimlott and the following staff and students from the Drama Section, School of Communications, University of South Australia, for their contribution to the recordings of the Listening tests: Kaye Lindberg, Myk Mykyta, Bruce Rosen, Don Telford, Geraldine Vallelonga, Amanda Fitzgerald, Amy Schutz, Katherine Figaira, Jo Gannon, Theresa Palma and Michelle Othams.

Thanks also go to Steve Martin for design assistance and technical support throughout the project, Neil Low, University of South Australia for recording and editing expertise, Evelyn Chefalachis and Heather Restall for typesetting, Greg Restall for website development, Steve Fuller for proof reading, Evasio Spagnuolo of Hyde Park Press for graphic design, Steve Martin for illustrations on pages 4, 11, 13, 21, 28, 33 and David Hardy for drawings on pages 81, 96 and 112, David Slater for initial Task 1 graphs, and Joanne Slater for the photographic image adapted for use in the cover design.

The authors are grateful to CELUSA and Language Australia for their support for this project.

The authors gratefully acknowledge the following for permission to use their material:
© Olympic Review, April-May 1999 issue for 'Balance and Imbalance in Children's Sport' by Lucio Bizzini (text page 88, 89); New Internationalist Magazine www.newint.org for 'Map Wars' adapted from an article by Peter Stalker in March 1989 (text page 50, 51); Freddy Silva and The Crop Circular www.lovely.clara.net. (text page 96, 97); David Suzuki for 'Are these two reporters on the same planet?' From: Earth Time Essays by, Stoddart Publications 1999. (text page 100, 101); Empire Publishing Company Ltd. for Team-based Learning by Inu Sengupta. TransWorld Education, volume 6, issue 3 (text page 64, 65); University of Cincinatti for 'Please Hold – not always music to your ears' by Marianne Kunnen-Jones, Research News Archive February 1999 (text page 56, 57); © National Sleep Foundation, 2002 www.sleepfoundation.org (text page 68, 69) for 'Sleeping on the job'; © The Australian Magazine and The Weekend Australian for 'Froggies go a woo-ing' 27/28 Nov. 1999 by Victoria Laurie (text page 80, 81). Other listening, reading, and writing test material not identified above was freshly written for test practice by the authors using information from a variety of spoken and written source material including ABC Australia and New Internationalist.

While the authors have made every effort to contact copyright holders, it has not been possible to identify the sources of all the material used. The authors and publisher would in such instances welcome information from copyright holders to rectify any errors or omissions.

CONTENTS

INTRODUCTION

UNIT 1 LISTENING

UNIT 2 READING

UNIT 3 WRITING

Note: Activities and Sample Answer follow each Task.

UNIT 4 SPEAKING

APPENDIX

INTRODUCTION

WELCOME to IELTS on Track! This test practice and preparation book has complete IELTS practice tests and Fast Track strategy and activity sections. It has been written for candidates who are preparing for the IELTS Test (Academic) in order to enter an academic course in an English-speaking institution. It is designed both for independent study and for use as a classroom textbook, especially for courses with a focus on writing and speaking skills. IELTS on Track is not an official IELTS publication and, like most other practice and preparation books, is not endorsed officially by IELTS.

WHAT IS THE IELTS TEST?

IELTS (International English Language Testing System) is a widely used and recognised international Test of English administered by Cambridge EFOL, formerly the University of Cambridge Local Examinations Syndicate (UCLES), the British Council, and IDP Education Australia. There are two versions: Academic (for students wishing to study in an English-speaking university or college) and General Training (for entry to vocational programs, schools or for immigration).

IELTS tests four performance areas: Listening, Reading, Writing and Speaking.
All candidates receive a test score between 1 (lowest) and 9 (highest). Academic institutions set their own IELTS entry scores.

The IELTS test is taken in this sequence:

Listening	40 questions — 30 minutes (+ 10 minutes to transfer answers)
Academic Reading	40 questions based on three texts — 60 minutes
Academic Writing	2 essay tasks — 60 minutes
Speaking	a standardised interview in 3 parts lasting 11-14 minutes

The current IELTS Handbook, available from all IELTS test centres worldwide gives more detailed information about the test.

INSIDE THIS BOOK

IELTS on Track is divided into **four units** — Listening, Reading, Writing and Speaking.
Each unit contains IELTS practice tests and a *Fast Track* section.

IELTS PRACTICE TESTS

COMPLETE LISTENING TESTS

The CD recordings offer a wide variety of English accents - British, American, Australian, Canadian and Scottish. This is consistent with the international nature of the IELTS test and the need for candidates to accommodate varieties of English spoken at a natural speed.

COMPLETE READING TESTS

Topics that are interesting, durable and even controversial have been favoured for inclusion. The aim has been to encourage critical thinking and discussion in IELTS preparation classrooms. All six tests are at a level comparable to the actual IELTS but the later tests pose a slightly higher level of challenge than the earlier ones.

COMPLETE WRITING TESTS

The Writing Test Task 2 prompts are usually short and clear. The aim has been to enable users of this book to focus on their own writing needs.

COMPLETE SPEAKING TESTS

The two sample IELTS Speaking tests on CD1 and CD2 are based on the **REVISED post – July 2001 test format.**

FAST TRACK SECTIONS

The FOUR Fast Track sections offer easy-to-follow strategies, activities and support.

LISTENING and READING

Immediately following both Listening and Reading test sections you will find the Fast Track sections. Refer to these pages to help you to analyse your mistakes and develop strategies for listening to and reading IELTS test material. Also check the student comments and language tips.

WRITING

The first part of this section explores the requirements of the IELTS Academic Writing Test and targets problem areas with hints for improvement. Each of the twelve Writing Tasks has planning assistance plus a Sample Answer, which generate language building activities. 'Notes' following the answers provide additional discourse pointers. Our belief is that IELTS candidates will become better attuned to the type of writing required for the test if they work analytically and interactively with whole sample answers. This is consistent with an inductive approach.

SPEAKING

This section has been designed for the requirements of the NEW Speaking Test (post 2001). Two recorded speaking tests on CDs are accompanied by listening activities so you can 'track' in an active way the interview format and content. There are also teacher comments for the two candidates, examiners' suggestions, plus extra test practice topics and questions.

HOW TO USE THIS BOOK

Of course, if you are working alone you will choose how best to use the book, but we would remind you of two principles that we hope may influence you.

Learn by reviewing performance

Our approach is based on an inductive view of learning. This means that we believe that it is better to learn by doing an IELTS test and then reviewing the strengths and weaknesses of your performance. Repeating the test helps to reinforce corrections and build confidence and speed. Your progress will be more efficient working this way than just doing one test after another.

'Use it or lose it'

Again, we strongly encourage you to try the same test several times to make sure you can build on what you have learnt about your performance, monitor and then demonstrate improvement. This is why we say 'Use it or lose it'.

You will find further guidance on how to use the book in each of the 4 Units.

GOOD LUCK!

UNIT 1 LISTENING

WHAT'S AHEAD...
IN THE LISTENING UNIT

- **The IELTS Listening Test**

- **Instructions for Test Practice**

- **Listening Tests 1-4**

- *Fast Track Listening*

    - **Learn from your mistakes**

    - **How can I improve?**

    - **Tips from test-takers**

THE IELTS LISTENING TEST

WHAT SHOULD I KNOW ABOUT IT?

Structure of the test

The test has 4 sections of increasing difficulty:

Section   1: a conversation on a general topic with 2 or 3 speakers.

2: a talk by one speaker on a general topic.

3: a conversation on an academic topic with 2 or 3 speakers.

4: a talk or lecture in academic style.

Questions

There are 40 questions, made up of 7 different question types.

Pauses

Within each section there are two short pauses, one at the beginning and one in the middle. These give you time to read questions before listening. There is also time at the end of each section to finish writing your answers.

Time

The listening test takes 30 minutes. You hear the recording ONCE only.

Test Instructions

There are recorded instructions at the beginning of the test. As you listen, write your answers on the question paper. At the end of the test you are given time to transfer the answers to an answer sheet.

INSTRUCTIONS FOR TEST PRACTICE

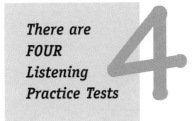

There are
FOUR
Listening
Practice Tests

Before You Start
Make a photocopy of the question paper or write your answers in the book. Use pencil.

Practise Under Test Conditions
Time: 30 minutes
Find a quiet place where you will not be interrupted.
DO NOT use a dictionary.
There are instructions for the test at the beginning of each CD.
Test 1 starts on CD 1 track 01.
Do not stop your player once you begin the test.

After You Finish
Practise transferring your answers to the Sample Answer Sheet on page 122.
Check the Answer Key on page 199.

Before You Try The Next Test
Turn to **FAST TRACK** *LISTENING* on page 35.

Repeat For Listening Tests 2 to 4.

SECTION 1   Questions 1–10

Questions 1–5
Circle the correct letter **A–D.**

> **EXAMPLE**   Andrea is feeling happy because...
>
> A   she's seen Harry.
> (B)   she's finished her exams.
> C   she can sleep in.
> D   Harry wants some advice.

[1]   What is Harry's problem?

A   He doesn't want to go back to England.
B   He needs to decide what to do with his possessions.
C   He wants to take everything to England.
D   He wants Andrea to buy his things.

[2]   Which of the items below does Harry want to sell?

  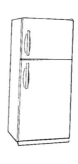 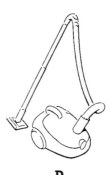

A   B   C   D

[3]   Where is Harry going to advertise his books for sale?

A   In the uni bookshop.
B   In the student newspaper.
C   In the department store.
D   In the economics department.

[4] Andrea thinks it is unlikely students will buy the furniture because...

    A   they're too poor.
    B   they live at home.
    C   it's the summer vacation.
    D   it's too expensive.

[5] Andrea thinks that a second hand shop...

    A   may not pay well.
    B   may not take your goods.
    C   may not like you.
    D   may not come on time.

Questions 6–10

*Complete Harry's notes using **NO MORE THAN TWO WORDS**.*

THINGS TO DO:

☐ **[6]** .... furniture etc in Trading Post.

☐ **[7]** .... or sell kitchen things.

☐ Get **[8]** ....first from second hand shop.

☐ Give clothes to **[9]** .... shop.

☐ **[10]** .... fridge and microwave to Andrea.

*Complete the Fitness Centre brochure using **NO MORE THAN TWO WORDS**.*

Sevenoaks
HEALTH & FITNESS CENTRE

Located conveniently at the **[11]** .... of Marion Street and Giles Street.

WE ARE OPEN FOR YOU
Monday – Friday **[12]** ....6..... am to 9.30 pm
Saturday   9.00 am to 4.00 pm
Sunday   9.00 am to **[13]** ....2...... pm

WET AREA

Aqua aerobic **[14]** ....for all ages and levels.

[15] ....lessons on weekday afternoons and weekend mornings.

SUPER CIRCUIT CLASSES

A cardio workout class that is easy to **[16]** ....

AEROBIC & STEP CLASSES
Aerobics room holds over 55 participants.

LARGE WELL-EQUIPPED GYM

Have a personal fitness assessment & individual **[17]** .... to suit you.

CARDIO-VASCULAR ROOM
Use the treadmills, bikes and steppers to burn fat, increase fitness, warm up.

Watch your favourite **[18]** .... while you exercise.

TWO FOR ONE SPECIAL MEMBERSHIP PLUS [19] ....**TRIAL OFFER**

ONLY $110 each for a whole **[20]** .... months! Get ready for summer.

HURRY, OFFER ENDS SOON!

SECTION 3   Questions 21–30

Questions 21–25

Complete the notes below using ONE WORD ONLY.

THE CANADIAN
FOOD MARKET

- Understanding subtle **[21]** .... between the Canadian and United States food sectors is important for successful food marketing

- Canada has many different ethnic groups: eg Toronto has large **[22]** .... and Asian populations

- Growth of ethnic specialities of Mediterranean, Caribbean, South East Asian and **[23]** .... foods

- Therefore demand is increasing for new **[24]** .... to prepare these foods plus condiments and sauces

- 80% of Canadian market controlled by 8 major national chains

- Seminar to compare Canadian food trends with **[25]** .... and UK

Complete the table below. Write **ONE WORD OR A NUMBER** for each answer.

THE CANADIAN
RETAIL FOOD SECTOR

TREND	COMMENTS
INTEREST IN HEALTHY FOOD	• Salads are the third most commonly eaten food in Canadian **[26]** .... • Most shoppers check **[27]** .... and nutritional information
NEW WAY OF LABELLING MEAT	• Labelled according to **[28]** .... technique eg simmering steak
'MOBILE MEALS'	• More meals eaten away from home • **[29]** .... increase in sales of snacks projected over next 3 years • Growth in **[30]** .... snacks such as muesli bars

10/10

SECTION 4   Questions 31–40

*Complete the lecture notes using **NO MORE THAN THREE WORDS** for each answer.*

PUBLIC SPEAKING

Public speaking means speaking to **[31]** .... people

Lack of confidence usually due to **[32]** ....

A. PLANNING

First part of public speaking is **[33]** ....

This includes: **[34]** .... and length of talk

Make speech notes on small cards to talk from

[35] .... with the audience (very important)

B. VOICE

Speak slowly – this gives time for pronunciation and is easier for audience

– bigger audience requires **[36]** .... speech

Project your voice – rehearse and **[37]** ....

Check intonation: varied tone and rhythm gives **[38]** ....

C. BODY LANGUAGE

Lastly, think about your **[39]** .... and gestures

Show confidence by: head up, chin out, shoulders back

Avoid scratching and fiddling because this **[40]** ....
and irritates your audience

SECTION 1   Questions 1–11

Questions 1–5

Complete the form below. Write **NO MORE THAN TWO WORDS OR A NUMBER** *for each answer.*

STUDENT EMPLOYMENT BUREAU

STUDENT REGISTRATION FORM

Faculty:	*Science*	**EXAMPLE**
Given Name:	Charlotte	
Surname:	[1]	
Address:	[2] .... Heathfield St, Maryland	
Telephone numbers:		
Home:	N/A	
Mobile:	[3]	
Number of hours preferred:	[4] .... per week	
Employment Experience:	[5]	

Questions 6–8

Circle the correct letter **A–D.**

[6] What time should Annetta finish work in the hamburger shop?

    A   7.00 pm
    B   7.00 am
    C   11.00 pm
    D   3.00 am

[7] What is the problem with Annetta's pay at the hamburger shop?

    A   the pay is too much
    B   the pay is late
    C   the pay isn't enough
    D   the pay isn't correct

[8] How many children will Annetta have to look after?

    A   two boys and a girl
    B   two boys and two girls
    C   four boys
    D   two girls and a boy

Questions 9–11

Label the map, choosing your answers from the list below.
*Write the correct letters **A–E** on the map.*

    A   Post Office
    B   Bank
    C   Primary School
    D   Petrol Station
    E   Kindergarten

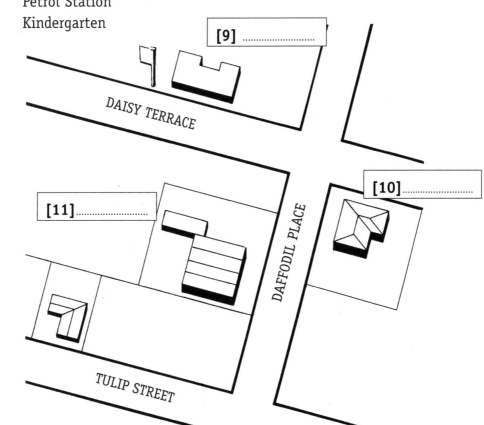

SECTION 2   Questions 12–21

Questions 12–14
Circle the correct letter A–D.

[12] The excursion is being organised for...

 A   all students.
 B   overseas students.
 C   new students.
 D   history students.

[13] How far is it from the college to Ironbridge?

 A   45 kilometres
 B   55 kilometres
 C   15 kilometres
 D   50 kilometres

[14] Students going on the excursion should look at the list and...

 A   print their telephone number and sign their name.
 B   print their name and tick if they have a car.
 C   print their name only if they have a car.
 D   print their name, telephone number, student number and tick if they have a car.

Questions 15–16
*Write **NO MORE THAN THREE WORDS OR NUMBERS** for each answer.*

[15] If students do not like eating meat, can they get a cheap meal at the restaurant in Ironbridge?

....

[16] What time must the students arrive to catch the bus?

....

Question 17

*Circle the correct letter **A–D**.*

[17] Which building is the bus garage?

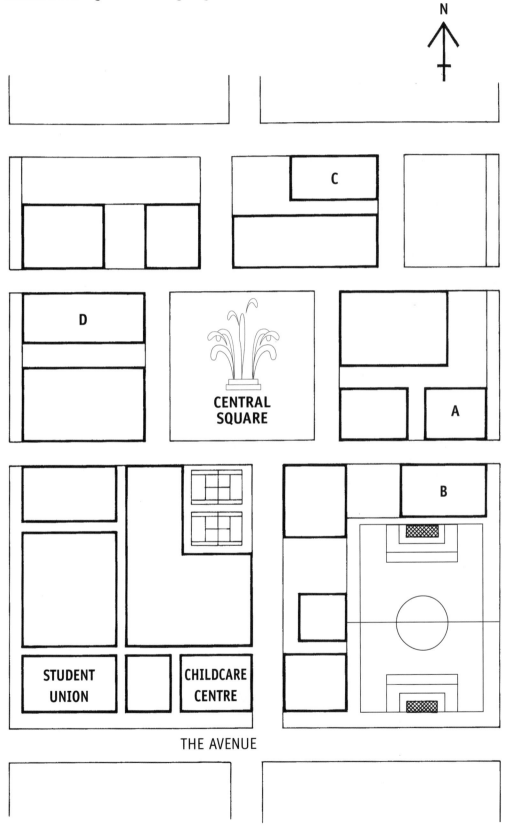

Questions 18–21

Write **NO MORE THAN FOUR WORDS OR NUMBERS** *for each answer.*

[18] Name **THREE** things that Pamela Sutcliffe recommends the students take on the excursion.

DON'T FORGET

☐ Comfortable Shoes

☐ Warm Jacket

☐

☐

☐

[19] Where will students find details in writing on Monday?

....

[20] Why is Ironbridge famous?

....

[21] Which three of the following famous tourist sights are mentioned?
Write the correct letters **A–H.**

A	Great Wall of China	**E**	Taj Mahal
B	Angkor Wat	**F**	Mt. Kilimanjaro
C	Grand Canyon	**G**	Leaning Tower of Pisa
D	Pyramids	**H**	Great Barrier Reef

SECTION 3 Questions 22–30

Questions 22–26

Look at this notice detailing the students' work experience placements. Write **NO CHANGE** if the information has **NOT** changed or **WRITE IN THE CHANGES**.

STUDENT NAME	BUSINESS	DAY am / pm	STARTING DATE	ANSWER
Theresa	University Book Shop	Friday mornings	23/3	**EXAMPLE** No change
Manuel	Mainly Music	Tuesday mornings	7/3	**EXAMPLE** Friday afternoons
Henry	The Beauty Shop	Thursday afternoons	22/3	[22] ....
Jo	Highway Hotels	Monday mornings	5/3	[23] ....
Nancy	Explore Travel Service	Wednesday mornings	14/3	[24] ....
Chris	Gorgeous Gowns	Wednesday mornings	14/3	[25] ....
Gordon	Games to Go!	Tuesday afternoons	20/3	[26] ....

Complete Gordon's notes about his work experience placement using **NO MORE THAN THREE WORDS OR A NUMBER.**

WORK EXPERIENCE PLACEMENT

Starting times **[27]** ....am

...........................pm

If ill, phone **[28]** ....

Presentation:

- due in week 10

- worth **[29]** .... of assessment

- outline history, management structure etc

- include visuals
  eg **[30]** .... and ....

SECTION 4   Questions 31–40

Questions 31–34

*Circle **T** for 'True' or **F** for 'False'.*

EXAMPLE		
The speaker has come from the Theosophical Society	T	Ⓕ

[31] One of the main points of the talk is to save money.   T   F

[32] She thinks students should do more housework.   T   F

[33] She argues that plastic containers won't biodegrade quickly.   T   F

[34] She warns that asthma sufferers should be careful with her recipes.   T   F

Questions 35–37

*Circle the correct letter **A-D.***

[35] To remove tea or coffee stains you should use...

   A   bicarbonate of soda.
   B   soda water.
   C   salt.
   D   any of these products.

[36] If you burn your saucepan accidentally, you should...

   A   throw it away.
   B   wipe it with vinegar.
   C   put vinegar and salt in it and boil it.
   D   put it in the fridge with bicarbonate of soda.

[37] If you scratch wooden furniture, you can remove the marks using...

    A   olive oil.

    B   sesame oil.

    C   olive oil and vinegar.

    D   wine vinegar.

Questions 38–40

*Complete the notes on the bottle label. Write **NO MORE THAN TWO WORDS** for each answer.*

'Green'
CARPET SHAMPOO

INGREDIENTS

PURE SOAP, CLOUDY AMMONIA, WASHING SODA

[38] ....

INSTRUCTIONS

MIX INGREDIENTS TOGETHER AND APPLY TO THE CARPET.

[39] ....UNTIL IT LATHERS.

WIPE OFF **[40]** ....

SECTION 1   Questions 1–10

Questions 1–6
*Complete the form using **NO MORE THAN THREE WORDS** for each answer.*

Buying a Used Car: Contact Details

Model:	*Celica*
Year:	*1985* **EXAMPLE**

Number of Owners:	**[1]**	....
Condition:		*overall good.*
	[2]	.... *done last year.*
Reason for Selling:	**[3]**	....
Asking Price:	**[4]**	....
Appointment Time:	**[5]**	....
Address:	**[6]**	.... , *Parkwood.*
Contact name:		*Elena*

Questions 7–10

*Circle the correct letter **A-D**.*

[7] What happened to Sam's car?

    A   It was damaged in an accident.
    B   It broke down.
    C   It was stolen.
    D   Sam sold it.

[8] Why does Jan need a car?

    A   She lives too far from the university.
    B   She uses it for her job.
    C   She spends too much time on the bus.
    D   She would feel safer at night with a car.

[9] What does Sam recommend?

    A   check the service records
    B   ask about the mileage
    C   get a mechanical inspection
    D   avoid buying an old car

[10] How are they travelling to Elena's?

    A   on foot
    B   on a motorcycle
    C   by bus
    D   on bicycles

Questions 11–13

As you listen, fill in the details to complete the information on the map below.

Trip takes **[11]** ....

Start here

Watch for Orcas here

[12] ....
often seen in
this area

Look for bears and
eagles along the inlet.

Stop at **[13]** .... for 1 hour

Questions 14–16

Fill in the chart using **NO MORE THAN THREE WORDS.**

Whale Identification Chart			
	Colour	Size	General Characteristics
Dolphins	grey	1 – 2 metres	[14] ....
Orcas/ Killer Whales	[15]	7 – 8 metres	• fierce hunters • eat fish, seals, other whales
Grey Whales	grey	[16]	• migratory • solitary • filter feeders, eat shrimp

Questions 17–20

Complete the following using **NO MORE THAN THREE WORDS.**

Advice for Participants on Whale Watching Excursions

- For a smooth ride, sit **[17]** .... of the boat.

- Watch the waves and hold onto the ropes.

- Survival suits are **[18]** .... in colour for maximum visibility.

  They are designed to keep you floating upright in the water even if you

  [19] .... and will protect you from the cold.

- For seasickness:

  Place a patch **[20]** .... instead of taking pills.

SECTION 3 Questions 21–30

Questions 21–23

*Fill in the summary below with **NO MORE THAN TWO WORDS OR A NUMBER** for each space.*

Selection Process for 'Travel Documentary'

- 34 interviewed from **[21]** .... applicants nationally

- 13 chosen for a **[22]** .... training course in film-making

- **[23]** .... finalists selected as competitors

Questions 24–26

*Complete the summary. Write **NO MORE THAN THREE WORDS** for each space.*

Requirements of competitors:

- produce a **[24]** .... every two weeks

- no previous professional **[25]** .... experience allowed

- make their own **[26]** .... and obtain approval

Questions 27 and 28

*Circle the correct letter **A–D**.*

[27] What was Sarah Price's worst experience during the trip?

    A   She got lost in Mongolia.
    B   She was injured in an accident.
    C   She got sick in a remote place.
    D   She was homesick.

[28] In which of the following areas does Ray expect to have most difficulty?

    A   communication in foreign languages
    B   time pressure
    C   organisation skills
    D   loneliness

Questions 29 and 30

*Write **NO MORE THAN TWO WORDS** for each answer.*

[29] In what month does the journey begin?

....

[30] Name 2 things that are provided free of charge to the competitors.

.... and ....

SECTION 4   Questions 31–40

Questions 31–33

*Circle the correct answer **A–D**.*

[31]   What does QWERTY stand for?

    A   the inventor of the typewriter
    B   the company that made the first typewriter
    C   letters on the home row of the keyboard
    D   letters on the top row of the keyboard

[32]   The first commercial typewriter was developed in...

    A   Germany.
    B   Japan.
    C   United States.
    D   Great Britain.

[33]   The purpose of the QWERTY keyboard layout was...

    A   to slow down typing speed.
    B   to prevent keys from sticking.
    C   to balance left and right hand use.
    D   to reduce typing inefficiency.

Questions 34–39

*Complete the summary below. Write **NO MORE THAN THREE WORDS** for each answer.*

In 1932 August Dvorak solved the inefficiency problem by re-designing the

[34] .... of the typewriter. He put the most commonly used letters on the

home row. Using the Dvorak keyboard, over 3000 words or **[35]** .... of all

work can be done from the home row. In contrast, only **[36]** .... can be

typed from the home row on the Qwerty keyboard. Other advantages of the Dvorak keyboard

include a 50% improvement in **[37]** .... and a 15 – 20% increase in

[38] .... But the most important difference is in finger movement.

Typists using the QWERTY keyboard moved their fingers **[39]** .... miles

per day compared to one mile a day for Dvorak typists.

Question 40

*Circle the correct letter **A–D**.*

Which of the following was the main reason why the Dvorak keyboard was never adopted?

A   the Depression of 1929
B   bad publicity
C   poor marketing
D   resistance to change

SECTION 1   Questions 1–10

Question 1

*Circle the correct letter **A–D.***

EXAMPLE

What time is it now as Jenny is talking to the agent?

A	11.00
B	11.30
C	12.00
D	12.30

---

[1]   Jenny's journey began in ...

A	London.
B	Singapore.
C	Sydney.
D	Hong Kong.

Questions 2–4

*Complete the form. Write **NO MORE THAN THREE WORDS** for each answer.*

Lost luggage CLAIM FORM

Name: *Jenny Lee*

Address: **[2]** .... *St., Riverside*

Telephone Number: **[3]** ....

Arrived on: *Flight QA 392*

Connecting from: Flight **[4]** ....

Questions 5–7

*Circle the correct letters **A–D**.*

[5]   Which of the drawings resembles Jenny's bag?

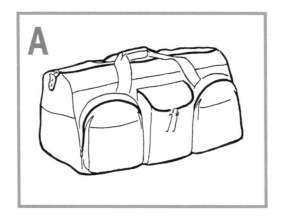

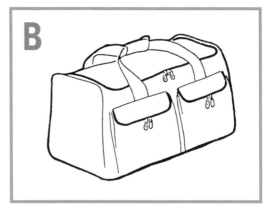

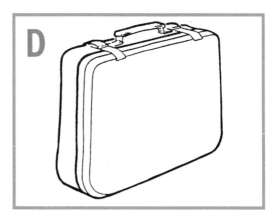

[6]   Which extra feature does Jenny identify?

    A   black colour
    B   wheels
    C   a red strap on the handle
    D   a metal handle

[7]   What time should Jenny's bag arrive?

    A   5.50 pm
    B   6.15 pm
    C   7.15 pm
    D   7.50 pm

Question 8
*Write **NO MORE THAN TWO WORDS** for the answer.*

When Jenny picks up the bag she has to **[8]** .... in person.

Questions 9 and 10
*Name **TWO** things that the agent advises Jenny to bring.*

[9] ....

[10] ....

SECTION 2   Questions 11–20

Questions 11 and 12
*Complete the notice below. Write **NO MORE THAN THREE WORDS OR A NUMBER** for each answer.*

ATS Ticketing Services

Box Office Hours (Regency Theatre):

Mon–Thurs: **[11]** ....

Friday, Saturday: 10 am – 8 pm

Internet Address: **[12]** ....

Questions 13–15

Indicate the number (1–4) to press for information on each of the following.

EXAMPLE	
	Answer
Tennis	1

[13] Symphony Orchestra ....

[14] Classical Ballet ....

[15] Formula One Grand Prix ....

Questions 16–20

*Fill in the information about **Formula One Grand Prix Tickets.***

FORMULA ONE GRAND PRIX TICKETS

Dates: [16] ....

Ticket prices:

Saturday (concession rate) [17] ....

Grandstand ticket (4 days) [18] ....

Gate opening time Saturday and Sunday: [19] ....

Booking fee per ticket: [20] ....

SECTION 3   Questions 21–30

Questions 21–23

Match the 3 speakers (21–23) with the background information below (A–G).

[21]   Anna   ....

[22]   Veronika   ....

[23]   Chris   ....

COMMITTEE MEMBERS' BACKGROUND AND EXPERIENCE

A	has done film reviews
B	currently in third year
C	gaining course credit for festival project
D	has made films
E	enrolled in Media Studies
F	works as a journalist
G	has film club experience

Question 24

Circle the correct letter A–D.

[24]   The total number of films in the festival each year is...

    A   five
    B   ten
    C   twelve
    D   sixteen

Questions 25–28

Circle the correct letter A–D.

[25]   Who chooses the films for the festival?

    A   the International Students' Society
    B   independent distributors
    C   a catalogue
    D   the committee members

[26] During the intermission, who is interviewed on camera?

    A   journalism students
    B   members of the audience
    C   a panel of experts
    D   the organising committee

[27] Of the films shown in the festival ...

    A   none is in English.
    B   most are dubbed.
    C   many have subtitles.
    D   some use both subtitles and dubbing.

[28] The festival did not make a profit last year because of...

    A   poor weather.
    B   high price of admission.
    C   lack of publicity.
    D   funding cuts by student council.

Question 29 and 30

Complete the following using **NO MORE THAN THREE WORDS**.

INTERNATIONAL FILM FESTIVAL
Planning Overview

Task:	To be completed by:
• **[29]**	1 March
• obtain sponsorship and advertising	15 March
• **[30]**	31 March
• print and distribute posters	April

SECTION 4   Questions 31–40

Questions 31–34

*Complete the summary using **NO MORE THAN ONE WORD** for each answer.*

Construction of a reed bed

- Rectangular hole 1 metre deep lined with **[31]** ....

- System of perforated tubing embedded in gravel

- **[32]** .... planted in bed

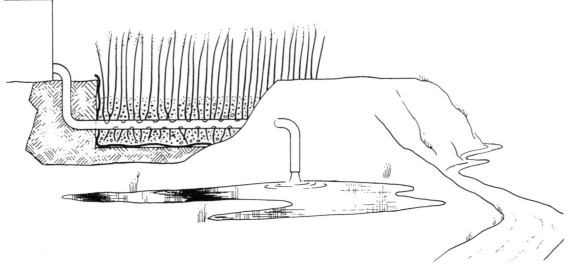

Process

- Sewage flows **[33]** .... from tank into reed bed.

- Oxygen from reeds combines with bacteria to reduce waste to elements.

- Water is **[34]** .... then released.

Questions 35–38

Complete the notes below. Write **NO MORE THAN THREE WORDS** for each answer.

Environmental benefits of reed beds

- produce good quality **[35]** .... for farming use

- provide a **[36]** .... for birds and animals

Advantages over conventional system

- lower **[37]** .... costs

- 10% cheaper installation

- less maintenance

- efficiency **[38]** .... with time

Questions 39 and 40

Write **NO MORE THAN ONE WORD** for each answer.

[39] Name **ONE** group which has opposed the introduction of reed bed technology.

....

[40] Give **ONE** concern about reed bed systems raised by students in the question period.

....

FAST TRACK LISTENING

LEARN FROM YOUR MISTAKES

Look again at your answers

You lose marks for small errors.
Mistakes like these can cost you easy marks.
Look at this example of an answer sheet.

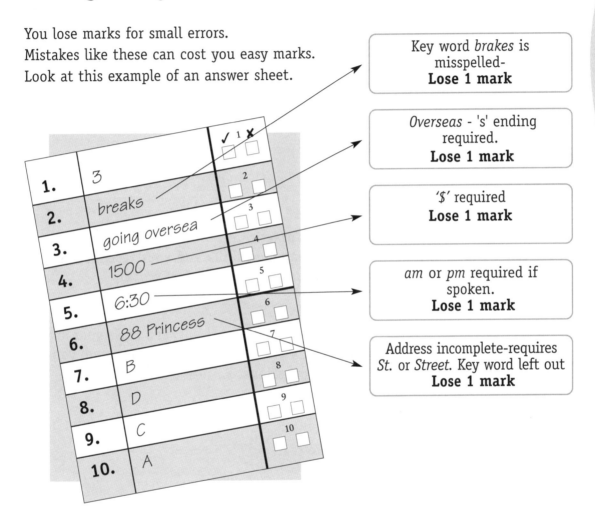

Key word *brakes* is misspelled-
Lose 1 mark

Overseas - 's' ending required.
Lose 1 mark

'$' required
Lose 1 mark

am or *pm* required if spoken.
Lose 1 mark

Address incomplete-requires *St.* or *Street*. Key word left out
Lose 1 mark

		✓ 1 ✗
1.	3	
2.	breaks	
3.	going oversea	
4.	1500	
5.	6:30	
6.	88 Princess	
7.	B	
8.	D	
9.	C	
10.	A	

Small and easily avoidable errors like these may mean the difference between getting your target score and having to re-sit the test. Look over your answers again. How many marks could you have saved?

Go back to the questions you got wrong

When checking your answers, mark an '**✗**' beside each question number you got wrong. If you are using pencil and writing in the book, erase your answers so you can use the tests again.

Review each question marked '✗'. Think about what you heard on the recording and how you chose your answer. Try to analyse each mistake.

Did you...

- ...not hear the information? Was it too fast...too complicated ...unclear?
- ...misunderstand the question?
- ...not have time to write the answer?
- ...make a careless mistake?

HOW CAN I IMPROVE?

Three times to get it right

Here's how to get the most from listening practice.
If you really want to improve both your language skills and your test results –
be prepared to do each test 3 times (unless you got a perfect score).

1
First Time
Check your score only. Don't read the correct answers. Erase your answers marked in pencil but leave an **✗** beside question numbers where you made an error. Pay attention to those **questions**. Re-read each one carefully.
Do not check the transcript.

2
Second Time
Leave a day, then **repeat the test**.
Check your answers.
How much did your score improve this time?
Which questions did you still get wrong? Do you know why?

3
Third Time
Listen to the recording. This time don't answer the questions, just **read the transcript** as you listen.
Underline **new vocabulary** - choose the words that seem most important.
Afterwards, go back, list the new words and use your dictionary to find the meaning.
Now check the questions you missed. Look for the answers in the underlined sections of the transcript.

By taking the time to repeat the tests, you are developing your listening skills, building vocabulary and increasing your understanding of test strategies. This is time well spent.

Make seconds count

Pauses

In a 30 minute listening, almost 4 minutes have no speaking at all. There are pauses after each section to finish writing your answers. But there are also important pauses at the beginning and in the middle of sections.

These pauses are your chance to prepare. They are the introduction to the topic. You can read the questions and get ready to answer.

What should I do in the pauses?

You can:
- underline key words in the instructions
- find out what the instructions tell you:
  about the speakers
  about the topic
- read the questions
- check question types
- predict/guess answers

Nawan thought his listening was weak but scored 6 on his first try.

'My best tip for listening is to use the 'pauses' to read the question paper really well. Don't just sit there waiting. Pick up information from the questions so you are ready to answer'.

More practice... with a friend

Do lots of training practice with dictation exercises. Ask an English-speaking friend to make up a list, based on the information below, and read it out to you. As you listen, write the words as quickly as you can, then check your answers.

For dictation:
- spelling of unknown words (eg surnames), note vowels and double letters
- telephone numbers, addresses, dates, times, amounts of money
- weights and measures (check a good grammar book for abbreviations - metric and imperial)

TIPS FROM TEST-TAKERS

We asked successful test-takers to help us list the keys to success in the listening test... and some things to watch out for. Here's what they came up with.

Warm up with English
'I warm up for test practice by putting on the radio (English language) as soon as I wake up in the morning. That helps me to start thinking in English.'

Keep calm
'Keep calm under pressure. I can hear more clearly and understand better when I'm relaxed.'

Tina scored 7 on the IELTS Listening Test

'I had a really bad start in the listening test. I couldn't understand one of the speakers - a strange accent and too fast. I started to panic and lost my place. Fortunately there was a pause. I breathed deeply, calmed myself down and got back on track. After that it seemed easier. So remember to breathe and don't panic if something unexpected happens.'

Keep track of questions
'Watch the question numbers so you don't get lost. Keep up with the questions so you know what to expect next. Don't fall behind.'

Stay interested
*'**Pay attention** to everything you hear. Listen as if every topic is really important and interesting - even if it isn't.'*

Anticipate
*'Predict what is coming next. Listen for those **'marker'** words that help you stay with the speaker.'*

Intelligent guessing
*'If you didn't get the answer, **guess**. Write something for each question. You can find a lot of useful information on the question paper - spelling, for example and sometimes even answers. Use your common sense.'*

Watch for the 'tricks'
*'You have to **keep listening**, even if you think you heard the answer. It can be a bit tricky, like in real life, where things have to be repeated and corrected. Be prepared.'*

Read, listen and write at the same time.
*'Take notes from anything you hear, to get used to listening and writing at the same time. Then, you have to **keep the questions in your mind** as well. Just keep **practising.** It gets easier.'*

UNIT 2 READING

WHAT'S AHEAD...
IN THE READING UNIT

- The IELTS Reading Test

- Instructions for Test Practice

- Reading Tests 1-4

- *Fast Track Reading*

  - Learn from your mistakes

  - How can I improve?

  - Tips from test-takers

THE IELTS READING TEST

WHAT SHOULD I KNOW ABOUT IT?

Structure of the test

The test has 3 reading passages of increasing difficulty.
The readings are based on those from magazines, books, journals or newspapers.
The topics are of general interest, written for a non-specialist audience.
At least one text contains a detailed logical argument.

Questions

There are 40 questions in total and 8 different question types.

Time

The reading test takes 1 hour.

Test Instructions

The instructions in each test are clear and easy to follow, and you are given examples of unfamiliar question types. You write your answers directly onto the reading answer sheet, not on your question paper. All answers get one mark.

INSTRUCTIONS FOR TEST PRACTICE

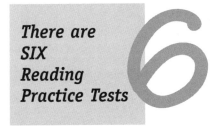

There are
SIX
Reading
Practice Tests

Before You Start

Make a photocopy of the Sample Answer Sheet on page 122 of this book. Use pencil.

Practise Under Test Conditions

Find a quiet place where you will not be interrupted.

DO NOT use a dictionary.

Set a timer for 1 hour.

After You Finish

Check the Answer Key on page 201.

Before You Try The Next Test

Turn to **FASTTRACK READING** on page 117.

Repeat for Reading Tests 2 to 6.

Passage 1

You should spend about 20 minutes on Questions 1–14 which are based on this passage.

Survivor from the sky

In a remarkable documentary, *Wings of Hope*, German director Werner Herzog recounts the true story of an eighteen year old girl, the sole survivor of a plane crash in the Amazon jungle in 1971. Twenty-nine years later Herzog returns to the jungle with Juliane Koepke, now a 46 year old biologist, and she tells her amazing story on film.

Juliane had just graduated from high school in Lima, Peru and, with her mother, was flying out to spend Christmas at her father's research station in the jungle. A half hour into the flight they encountered a horrific storm. In the midst of wild turbulence, the plane was struck by lightning and fell into a nose dive. Passengers screamed as baggage flew around the compartment. Then the plane broke into pieces and suddenly Juliane found herself outside free-falling 30,000 feet. 'I was suspended in mid-air, still in my seat. It wasn't so much that I had left the plane but that the plane had left me. It simply wasn't there any more. I was all alone with my row of seats,' says Juliane. 'I sailed on through the air, then I tumbled into a fall. The seatbelt squeezed my stomach and I couldn't breathe any more.' Before she lost consciousness, Juliane saw the dense jungle below, 'a deep green, like broccoli', with no clearings for hundreds of miles.

Somehow, miraculously, Juliane survived that fall from the sky. In the film, she speculates on a number of factors which may have combined to save her. First, the storm had produced a strong updraft from the thunder clouds. Secondly, being strapped into a row of seats, she was aware of falling in a spiralling movement, like a maple seed pod. Then, hitting the canopy of trees, she tumbled through a maze of vines which slowed her landing in deep mud.

But surviving the fall, though miraculous in itself, was just the beginning. When Juliane awoke hours later, wet and covered with mud, she was still strapped to her seat. Staggering to her feet, she assessed her injuries: a fractured bone in the neck, concussion and deep cuts in her leg and back. She was also in shock, lost and totally alone in the Amazon jungle.

No doubt it was her familiarity with the wilderness that enabled her to cope. Her parents were biologists and Juliane had grown up in the jungle. She realised her only hope was to follow a little stream of water nearby, trusting that it would eventually lead to a larger river and rescue. With no provisions, dressed in the miniskirt she had worn on the plane and wearing just one shoe, she set off through the jungle. She passed broken fragments from the plane - a wheel, an engine. 'Initially, I saw planes circling above me, but after a few days I realised the search had been called off,' she said.

Surprisingly she felt no hunger but as the days passed her health was deteriorating rapidly. The gash in her shoulder, where flies had laid their eggs was now crawling with maggots. 'I knew I'd perish in the jungle so I stayed in the water.' Walking in the stream however presented one risk more serious than any others. Before each step she had to poke ahead in the sand with a stick, to avoid treading on poisonous sting rays, lying hidden on the bottom.

As the stream grew into a river, swimming was the only option. However, here in deeper water, there were new threats. Crocodiles basking on the shores slipped silently into the water as she passed. Juliane trusted that they feared humans and were entering the water to hide. She swam on. On the tenth day, starving and barely conscious, she spotted a hut and a canoe. They belonged to three woodcutters working nearby. Rescue was at hand.

For this 46 year old woman, re-living such a traumatic experience on film must have been a great challenge. But she shows little emotion. Flying back into the jungle she sits in the same seat (19F) as on that fateful day. She is dispassionate, unemotional in describing the flight. On the ground, when they finally locate the crash site, in dense jungle, Juliane is scientific in her detachment, looking through the debris, now buried under dense vegetation. She examines a girl's purse, the skeleton of a suitcase. Walking along the stream, she spots the engine which she remembers passing on the third day. Her arms and legs are covered with mosquitoes, but she seems to ignore all discomfort. Then, back in the town, standing in front of a monument erected in memory of the victims of the crash, entitled *Alas de Esperanza* (Wings of Hope), Juliane comments simply, 'I emerged, as the sole embodiment of hope from this disaster.'

Questions 1–14

Questions 1–3

*Answer the following questions using **NO MORE THAN THREE WORDS** from the passage.*

[1]   How old was Juliane at the time of the crash?   ....

[2]   What is her occupation now?   ....

[3]   What was the cause of the plane crash?   ....

Questions 4–10

*Choose the correct letter **A–D**.*

[4]   What happened to the plane?

    A   It broke apart in the air.
    B   It hit trees and exploded.
    C   It crashed into a mountainside.
    D   It hit the ground and burst into flames.

[5]   Which of the following did **NOT** help to slow her fall?

    A   an updraft caused by storm clouds
    B   hitting vines
    C   the section of seats to which she was attached
    D   a parachute

[6]   Which of the following injuries did she sustain?

    A   a broken foot
    B   a broken arm
    C   concussion
    D   cuts on her head

[7]   What helped her to survive?

    A   knowledge of the jungle
    B   a map showing the location of the river
    C   appropriate clothing and shoes
    D   food supplies from the plane

[8] What was the biggest threat to her survival?

    A   infected wounds
    B   sting rays
    C   starvation
    D   crocodiles

[9] How long was she lost in the jungle?

    A   3 days
    B   5 days
    C   10 days
    D   15 days

[10] How was she finally rescued?

    A   A search party found her in the jungle.
    B   Native hunters found her.
    C   She signaled to a plane from the river.
    D   She reached a campsite along the river.

Questions 11–14

Do the following statements agree with the views of the writer in this passage?

Write:

YES	*if the statement agrees with the writer's views.*
NO	*if the statement contradicts the writer's views.*
NOT GIVEN	*if the information is not clearly given in the passage.*

[11] Other survivors of the crash were found in the jungle.

[12] Juliane was upset when she re-visited the crash site.

[13] *Wings of Hope* is the name given to a memorial statue.

[14] Juliane suffered nightmares for many years as a result of her experience.

Passage 2

You should spend about 20 minutes on Questions 15–27 which are based on this passage.

The race to make spider silk

The strength, toughness, and elasticity of silk continue to fascinate scientists, who wonder what gives this natural material its unusual qualities. Finer than human hair, lighter than cotton, and ounce for ounce stronger than steel, silk is of special interest to materials researchers. They are trying to duplicate its properties and synthesise it for large-scale production. Silk holds the promise of wear-resistant shoes and clothes; stronger ropes, nets, seatbelts and parachutes; rustfree panels and bumpers for automobiles; improved sutures and bandages; artificial tendons and ligaments; supports for weakened blood vessels as well as bulletproof vests.

Many insects secrete silks of varying quality. Best known is the moth *bombyx mori,* whose caterpillar is commonly known as the silkworm. It spins its cocoon from a single thread between 300 and 900 metres long and has been used for centuries to make fine garments. But the focus of scientific attention today is on spider silk: tougher, stretchier, and more waterproof than silkworm strands. Spiders make as many as seven different types of silk, but one spider and two types of silk are at the centre of intense interest. The spider is the golden orb-weaving spider, *nephila clavipes.* Its two silks under investigation go by the evocative names 'dragline' and 'capture'.

Dragline is the silk which forms the frame for the wheel-shaped webs and enables the dangling spider to drop down and grab its prey. This silk exhibits a combination of strength and toughness unmatched by high-performance synthetic fibre.

Capture silk is the resilient substance at the centre of the web. To catch a speeding insect, it may stretch to almost three times its original length. Insects get entangled in the sticky web because the stretchiness of capture silk lets the web move back and forth after the insect hits it. If the web were stiff, the insect might just bounce off. Whereas dragline is stronger, capture silk is more flexible, five times more flexible in fact.

Because the orb weaver's survival depends on its silk, some 400 million years of evolution have fine-tuned a remarkably tough and versatile material. Now, research groups all over the world are competing to spin the first artificial spider silk, a job that requires a three-step approach: to determine the fibre's molecular architecture, to understand the genes that yield silk proteins, and then to learn how to spin the raw material into threads.

The first two steps are well underway. The molecular structure for both dragline and capture silk is known and now researchers have cloned several genes for the silks and unravelled their protein structure.

The next step is to find hosts for the artificial genes. Plants and fungi, as well as bacteria, are being considered. If a hardy plant could express a dragline silk gene, silk proteins could eventually be harvested in large quantities, processed into a liquid polymer, and spun in factories. A different experimental approach is to insert the web gene into goats in order to collect the protein from the goats' milk. Goats are being used instead of the simpler and much cheaper bacteria, because the secret of the protein's strength lies in how the molecules cross-link with one another. When bacteria is used to make artificial web, the protein folds in a way that prevents it from cross-linking properly, resulting in hard white lumps. The spider makes protein in a manner similar to the way mammals make milk, so the researchers hope that the protein made in the goats' mammary glands will be able to cross-link properly. Once the protein is extracted from the goats' milk, the next step is to find a way to spin it.

Spiders make their silk in environmentally friendly ways. They process proteins from water-based solutions which, from a manufacturing point of view, is very attractive. The process of making synthetic fibres like nylon, on the other hand requires petroleum products or organic solvents and results in pollution. So biotechnologists are motivated by both the practical and economic potential of generating artificial spider silk. Globally, as much as 60 per cent of the threads used to weave clothing come from natural fibre, including cotton, wool, and silk. The aim is to offer substitutes for natural fibres that are free of the problems of poor wash-wear performance: stretching, wrinkling and shrinkage. They are seeking a better-than-natural alternative fibre for which there is a major market. Bio-inspired materials are providing a new frontier for the fibre business.

Questions 15–27

Questions 15–19

Classify the following as relating to:

    A   the silk of *bombyx mori*

    B   dragline silk of *nephila clavipes*

    C   capture silk of *nephila clavipes*

EXAMPLE		
	Answer	
forms the cocoon	A	

[15] forms the framework of a web

[16] most elastic silk

[17] allows predator to drop quickly

[18] single strand can be up to 900 metres long

[19] strongest silk

Questions 20–24

Do the following statements reflect the claims of the writer in the passage?

Write:

YES	*if the statement reflects the claims of the writer.*
NO	*if the statement contradicts the writer.*
NOT GIVEN	*if there is no information about this in the passage.*

[20] All spiders secrete silk.

[21] Artificial genes for spider silk have been produced.

[22] Spider silk protein occurs naturally in goats' milk.

[23] China is leading research efforts in the area of spider silk.

[24] Spider silk is now being produced commercially.

Questions 25–27

Using **NO MORE THAN THREE WORDS** from the passage for each answer, complete the following.

Comparison of Synthetic and Natural Fibres

- Main problem in the production of synthetic fibres:

  [25] ....

- **3** disadvantages of natural fibres:

  [26] ....

  ....

  ....

- Proportion of clothing made from natural fibre:

  [27] ....

Passage 3

You should spend about 20 minutes on Questions 28–40 which are based on this passage.

MAP WARS

A map of the world expresses a point of view. A correct model of the earth is a sphere–or an ellipsoid to be precise. Photographs of the earth from space provide comforting reassurance on that point. If you wish to know the relative positions of the continents and the oceans you should go out and buy yourself a globe and spin it around.

But a globe cannot be pinned to a wall or printed in a book. For that you need a two-dimensional representation. This is where the problems start since you cannot project three-dimensional information onto a flat plane without making certain assumptions. The arguments between cartographers mostly concern what those assumptions should be.

The simplest two-dimensional representation is a 'cylindrical' projection–what you get by wrapping a sheet of paper around a globe and simply transferring the information across. This means it indicates true north and south. So Newfoundland is directly north of Venezuela and it appears that way on the map. East and west similarly are also indicated correctly. Such a map demonstrates what is called 'fidelity of axis'.

One of the longest-lived cylindrical projections was based on the needs of sixteenth century navigators. Gerhard Kremer, a Flemish mathematician, produced his view of the world in 1569. 'Kremer' translates to 'merchant' in English and 'mercator' in Latin. And the Mercator projection survives to this day in many books and maps.

Mercator's projection of the world also shows intermediate compass directions like north-west more or less accurately. So it is possible to conclude from his map that Brazil is south-west of Liberia and if you plot a course in that direction you will eventually arrive at your destination. No wonder it was appreciated by the early explorers! If it can be used in this way a map is said to have 'fidelity of angle'.

But fidelity of angle is only achieved at a cost. To make it work, the further away you get from the equator the further apart you have to move the horizontal lines of latitude. As these distances increase so do the sizes of the countries underneath them. So by the time you get to the North or South Poles the lines would be drawn infinitely far apart and the Arctic and Antarctic regions can scarcely be represented at all since they would be infinitely large. More importantly the relative sizes of intermediate areas are completely distorted; South America seems smaller than Europe whereas in fact it is twice the size. These changes in scale distort both the size and shape of countries. Given such defects it is surprising that the Mercator projection has survived so long, especially as dozens of other more satisfactory projections have appeared since. One of the best known of these is the Aitoff projection of 1889, which attempted to represent country sizes and shapes more correctly. But to do so required a compromise–the lines of latitude and longitude had to be 'bent'. Fidelity of axis had thus been lost and you could no longer judge north, south, east and west so easily. Most of us however, did not notice that these projections were different from Mercator. We assumed that all maps were simply factual statements.

Dr Arno Peters, a German historian, was irritated by the maps he saw widely published, particularly by the survival of Mercator which he argued, gave a euro-centric view of the world. It shrank the developing countries since most of these are around the equator, and it expanded the richer countries since they lay further north. Even the equator itself is shown two-thirds of the way down on the traditional Mercator map. Dr Peters insisted that his map, which first appeared in 1985, has equal-area projection so that no country is given prominence over another, plus fidelity of axis to avoid the disorientating effect of bent lines of latitude and longitude.

Then there is the question of country shape. If you were to take a photo of a globe in its normal position you would find the countries around the equator like Zaire or Ecuador came out of it pretty well. They would be shown relatively large and with something close to their correct shape. But further north or south there are considerable distortions: Australia tails away alarmingly. Dr. Peters decided that the minimum distortions should occur not at the equator but at the 45 degree lines of latitude, as these are much more populated areas. However this controversial Peters map does radically change the shape of both Africa and South America; and although all projections distort to some extent, it is clear that Africa appears exceptionally long and thin on the Peters map.

But the oddity of the Peters projection is at least partly responsible for its success, as there has been widespread discussion on the misrepresentation of country sizes in previous maps. The issues which the Peters map raises are relatively simple. If you decide you want an equal area map with fidelity of axis you will always get something resembling the Peters projection. If you decide that shape is more significant you will get something else.

The real value of the Peters projection is that it has made the world think about something that before was never taken seriously: that maps of the world represent a point of view just as do press articles or TV programmes or photographs. But it isn't recommended that you navigate a '747' round the world with the Peters projection or with any other single global projection–they would all lead you astray!

Questions 28–40

Questions 28–31
Complete the summary. Choose your answers from the box below the summary. There are more words than you will need to fill the gaps.

EXAMPLE

For four centuries map makers have been trying to convert three-dimensional

information as ...*accurately*... as possible onto a two-dimensional plane. However,

each method of **[28]** .... involves a compromise. Thus Mercator's

projection indicates true north and south, known as fidelity of

[29] .... , but misrepresents the relative size of countries.

To avoid this distortion other cartographers rounded the lines of latitude and

longitude. Dr Peters felt that such maps presented a first-world

[30] .... His map, with equal area projection, enables us to

[31] .... the size of one country with another.

List of words

axis	estimate	perspective
map	direction	compare
size	judge	accurately
angle	distances	models
projection	change	

Questions 32–36

Use the information in the text to match the map projections **[M A P]** *with the characteristics listed below.*

M   Mercator projection

A   Aitoff projection

P   Peters projection

EXAMPLE	*Answer*
designed for the needs of early navigators	*M*

[32] makes Europe seem larger than it is

[33] maximum distortions at the poles

[34] maintains greatest accuracy at 45 degrees latitude

[35] most distorts the position of the equator

[36] more accurately represents country shapes and sizes

Questions 37–39

*Choose one drawing **(A–D)** to match each of the three projection types **(37–39)**. There are more drawings than names so you will not use all of them.*

[37] Mercator projection

[38] Aitoff projection

[39] Peters projection

A

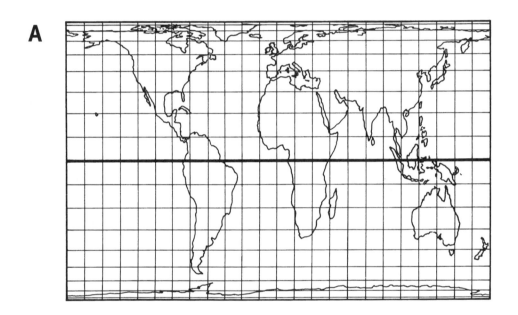

B

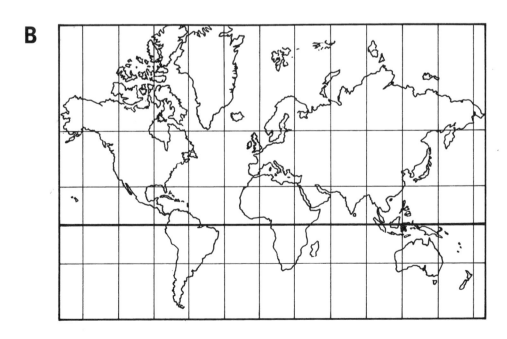

C

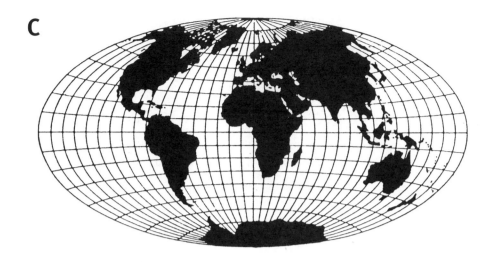

D

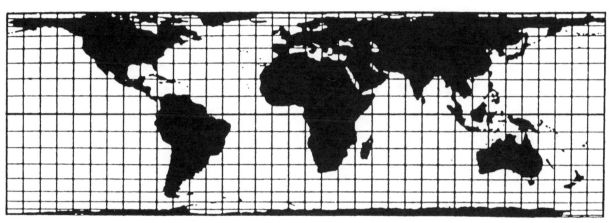

Question 40

Choose the correct letter **A–D**.

[40] The main point made by the writer of this article is that we need to...

    A   understand maps.

    B   understand map-making.

    C   understand that maps are not objective.

    D   understand the importance of latitude and longitude.

Passage 1

You should spend about 20 minutes on Questions 1–13 which are based on this passage.

PLEASE HOLD THE LINE

Nearly all of us know what it's like to be put on 'musical hold'. Call almost any customer service number, and you can expect to hear at least a few bars of boring elevator music before an operator picks up. The question is: do you hang up or do you keep holding? That may depend on your gender and what type of music is playing, according to research reported by University of Cincinnati Associate Professor of Marketing, James Kellaris.

Kellaris, who has studied the effects of music on consumers for more than 12 years, teamed with Sigma Research Management Group to evaluate the effects of 'hold music' for a company that operates a customer service line.

The researchers tested four types of 'on-hold' music with 71 of the company's clients, 30 of them women. Light jazz, classical, rock and the company's current format of adult alternative (a mix of contemporary styles) were all tested. The sample included individual consumers, small business and large business segments. Participants were asked to imagine calling a customer assistance line and being placed on hold. They were then exposed to 'on-hold' music via headsets and asked to estimate how long it played. Their reactions and comments were also solicited and quantified by the researchers.

Service providers, of course don't want you to have to wait on hold, but if you do, they want it to be a pleasant experience for you. But Kellaris' conclusions may hold some distressing news for companies. No matter what music was played, the time spent 'on hold' was generally overestimated. The actual wait in the study was 6 minutes, but the average estimate was 7 minutes and 6 seconds.

He did find some good news for the client who hired him. The kind of music they're playing now, alternative, is probably their best choice. Two things made it a good choice. First, it did not produce significantly more positive or negative reactions in people. Second, males and females were less polarised in their reactions to this type of music.

Kellaris' other findings, however, make the state of musical hold a little less firm: time spent 'on hold' seemed slightly shorter when light jazz was played, but the effect of music format differed for men and women. Among the males, the wait seemed shortest when classical music was played. Among the females, the wait seemed longest when classical music was played. This may be related to differences in attention levels and musical preferences.

In general, classical music evoked the most positive reactions among males; light jazz evoked the most positive reactions (and shortest waiting time estimates) among females. Rock was the least preferred across both gender groups and produced the longest waiting time estimates. 'The rock music's driving beat kind of aggravates people calling customer assistance with a problem' said Kellaris. 'The more positive the reaction to the music, the shorter the waiting time seemed to be. So maybe time does tend to fly when you're having fun, even if you're on musical hold', Kellaris joked.

But unfortunately for companies operating on-hold lines, men and women have different ideas about what music is 'fun'. 'The possible solution', Kellaris joked, 'might be for the recorded message to say: if you're a male, please press one; if your a female, please press two. If you are in a bad mood, please hang up and try later.'

Questions 1–13

Questions 1–2
Choose the correct letter A–D.

[1]   The researchers concluded that …

   A   subjects underestimated the time spent 'on hold'.
   B   it is better for companies not to use any 'on-hold' music.
   C   light jazz was the most acceptable music overall.
   D   both gender and type of music influence callers' reaction.

[2]   The researchers recommended that …

   A   their client continue to play alternative music.
   B   four types of music should be offered to people 'on hold'.
   C   advertising is preferable to music.
   D   women can be kept waiting for longer than men.

Questions 3–7
Choose the type of music from the list A–D below which corresponds to the findings of the study.

Types of music

A   light jazz

B   alternative

C   classical

D   rock

[3] music preferred by men

[4] longest waiting time estimate (both sexes)

[5] music to avoid on telephone hold

[6] music to use if clients are mostly women

[7] best choice of 'on-hold' music overall

Questions 8–13

Do the following statements agree with the claims of the writer?

Write:

YES	*if the statement agrees with the claims of the writer.*
NO	*if the statement contradicts the writer.*
NOT GIVEN	*if it is impossible to say what the writer thinks about this.*

[8] Businesses want to minimise the time spent 'on hold'.

[9] The research sample consisted of real clients of a company.

[10] The sample consisted of equal numbers of men and women.

[11] Advertising is considered a poor alternative to 'on-hold' music.

[12] The consumer service company surveyed was playing classical music.

[13] Researchers asked subjects only to estimate the length of time they waited 'on hold'.

Passage 2

You should spend about 20 minutes on Questions 14–25 which are based on this passage.

Did tea and beer bring about industrialisation?

A   Alan Macfarlane thinks he could rewrite history. The professor of anthropological science at King's College, Cambridge has, like other historians, spent decades trying to understand the enigma of the Industrial Revolution. Why did this particular important event–the world-changing birth of industry–happen in Britain? And why did it happen at the end of the 18th century?

B   Macfarlane compares the question to a puzzle. He claims that there were about 20 different factors and all of them needed to be present before the revolution could happen. The chief conditions are to be found in history textbooks. For industry to 'take off,' there needed to be the technology and power to drive factories, large urban populations to provide cheap labour, easy transport to move goods around, an affluent middle-class willing to buy mass-produced objects, a market-driven economy, and a political system that allowed this to happen. While this was the case for England, other nations, such as Japan, Holland and France also met some of these criteria. All these factors must have been necessary but not sufficient to cause the revolution. Holland had everything except coal, while China also had many of these factors. Most historians, however, are convinced that one or two missing factors are needed to solve the puzzle.

C   The missing factors, he proposes, are to be found in every kitchen cupboard. Tea and beer, two of the nation's favourite drinks, drove the revolution. Tannin, the active ingredient in tea, and hops, used in making beer, both contain antiseptic properties. This, plus the fact that both are made with boiled water, helped prevent epidemics of waterborne diseases, such as dysentery, in densely populated urban areas.

D   Historians had noticed one interesting factor around the mid-18th century that required explanation. Between about 1650 and 1740, the population was static. But then there was a burst in population. The infant mortality rate halved in the space of 20 years, and this happened in both rural areas and cities, and across all classes. Four possible causes have been suggested. There could have been a sudden change in the viruses and bacteria present at that time, but this is unlikely. Was there a revolution in medical science? But this was a century before Lister introduced antiseptic surgery. Was there a change in environmental conditions? There were improvements in agriculture that wiped out malaria, but these were small gains. Sanitation did not become widespread until the 19th century. The only option left was food. But the height and weight statistics show a decline. So the food got worse. Efforts to explain this sudden reduction in child deaths appeared to draw a blank.

E This population burst seemed to happen at just the right time to provide labour for the Industrial Revolution. But why? When the Industrial Revolution started, it was economically efficient to have people crowded together forming towns and cities. But with crowded living conditions comes disease, particularly from human waste. Some research in the historical records revealed that there was a change in the incidence of waterborne disease at that time, especially dysentery. Macfarlane deduced that whatever the British were drinking must have been important in controlling disease. They drank beer and ale. For a long time, the English were protected by the strong antibacterial agent in hops, which were added to make beer last. But in the late 17th century a tax was introduced on malt. The poor turned to water and gin, and in the 1720s the mortality rate began to rise again. Then it suddenly dropped again. What was the cause?

F Macfarlane looked to Japan, which was also developing large cities about the same time, and also had no sanitation. Waterborne diseases in the Japanese population were far fewer than those in Britain. Could it be the prevalence of tea in their culture? That was when Macfarlane thought about the role of tea in Britain. The history of tea in Britain provided an extraordinary coincidence of dates. Tea was relatively expensive until Britain started direct trade with China in the early 18th century. By the 1740s, about the time that infant mortality was falling, the drink was common. Macfarlane guesses that the fact that water had to be boiled, together with the stomach-purifying properties of tea so eloquently described in Buddhist texts, meant that the breast milk provided by mothers was healthier than it had ever been. No other European nation drank tea so often as the British, which, by Macfarlane's logic, pushed the other nations out of the race for the Industrial Revolution.

G But, if tea is a factor in the puzzle, why didn't this cause an industrial revolution in Japan? Macfarlane notes that in the 17th century, Japan had large cities, high literacy rates and even a futures market. However, Japan decided against a work-based revolution, by giving up labour-saving devices, even animals, to avoid putting people out of work. Astonishingly, the nation that we now think of as one of the most technologically advanced, entered the 19th century having almost abandoned the wheel. While Britain was undergoing the Industrial Revolution, Macfarlane notes wryly, Japan was undergoing an industrious one.

H The Cambridge academic considers the mystery solved. He adds that he thinks the UN should encourage aid agencies to take tea to the world's troublespots, along with rehydration sachets and food rations.

Questions 14–25

Questions 14–18

*The passage has 8 sections **A–H**.*
*Choose the most suitable headings for paragraphs **B–F** from the list of headings below.*
*Write the appropriate numbers **(i–x)**.*
There are more headings than sections so you will not use all of them.

List of Headings

(i)	The significance of tea drinking
(ii)	Possible solution to the puzzle
(iii)	Industry in Holland and France
(iv)	Significant population increase
(v)	The relationship between drinks and disease
(vi)	Gin drinking and industrialisation
(vii)	Dysentery prevention in Japan and Holland
(viii)	Japan's waterborne diseases
(ix)	Preconditions necessary for industrial revolution
(x)	Introduction

EXAMPLE	Answer
Section **A**	**x**

[14]   Section **B**

[15]   Section **C**

[16]   Section **D**

[17]   Section **E**

[18]   Section **F**

Questions 19–22

Complete the table using **NO MORE THAN THREE WORDS** from the passage.

CENTURY	SOCIAL CHANGE IN BRITAIN	REASON	EFFECT ON POPULATION
mid 17th century	main drinks were still *beer and ale* **EXAMPLE**	hops helped to make beer last longer	no significant change
late 17th century	gin becomes more popular, especially with poor people	beer becomes expensive because of [19]	mortality rate goes up
early 18th century	[20] .... drinking starts to become widespread	Britain starts trade with China	mortality rate goes down
mid 18th century	decline in urban deaths caused by [21]	[22] .... water used for tea and beer; antibacterial qualities of tannin	infant mortality rate goes down by half

Questions 23–25

Choose the correct letter **A–D**.

[23] In 1740 there was a population explosion in Britain because...

  A   large numbers of people moved to live in cities.
  B   larger quantities of beer were drunk.
  C   of the health-protecting qualities of beer and tea.
  D   of the Industrial Revolution.

[24] According to the author, the Japanese did not industrialise because they didn't ...

  A   like drinking beer.
  B   want animals to work.
  C   like using wheels.
  D   want unemployment.

[25] Macfarlane thinks he has discovered why...

  A   the British drink beer and tea.
  B   industrialisation happened in Britain when it did.
  C   the Japanese did not drink beer.
  D   sanitation wasn't widespread until the 19th century.

Passage 3

TEAM-BASED LEARNING

With the globalisation of information technology (IT) and worldwide access to the Internet, people from all areas of learning are finding themselves using some form of information technology in the workplace. The corporate world has seen a boom in the use of IT tools, but conversely, not enough people with IT skills that can enter the workplace and be productive with minimal on-the-job training.

A recent issue of the New York Times reports that many companies are looking for smart students who may have a budding interest in IT. Some companies, trying to encourage students to attend interviews, provide good salary packages and challenging work environments. For example, one American IT consulting company offers high salaries, annual bonuses, and immediate stock options to potential recruits. It also brings in 25 to 40 prospective applicants at a time for a two-day visit to the company. This time includes interviews, team exercises and social events. The idea behind the team exercises is that the applicants get to see that they will be working with other smart people doing really interesting things, rather than sitting alone writing code.

In the past 10 years, employers have seen marked benefits from collaborative projects in product development. Apart from the work environment, there is also a similar body of research indicating that small team-based instruction can lead to different kinds of desirable educational results. In order to prepare IT graduates to meet these workplace requirements, colleges and universities are also beginning to include team-based educational models.

One of the leaders in promoting team-based education is the American Intercontinental University (AIU), which has campuses world-wide. AIU offers programs in IT with a major portion of the curriculum based on team projects. AIU has a large body of international students and students from different educational backgrounds. This team-based learning gives the students a sense of social and technical support within the group, and allows students firsthand experience of both potential successes and of inherent problems encountered when working with others.

Team-oriented instruction has not been the common mode of delivery in traditional college settings. However, since most college graduates who choose to go into an IT work environment will encounter some form of teamwork at work, it is to their advantage that they are educated using collaborative learning and that they are taught the tools needed to work with different people in achieving common goals or objectives.

In team-based learning, students spend a large part of their in-class time working in permanent and heterogeneous teams. Most teams are made up of individuals with different socio-cultural backgrounds and varying skill levels. Team activities concentrate on using rather than just learning concepts, whilst student grades are a combination of overall team performance and peer evaluation of individual team members.

In a team-based environment, the teacher takes on the role of a facilitator and manager of learning, instead of just providing information to passive students. The facilitator/teacher also guides the team in identifying their goals and establishing standards of team performance. Team exercises then help the students to improve their problem-solving skills by applying theory to simulated real-world situations. Working as a team allows students to adopt new roles and empowers them to control their own learning. Students in teams are taught to use each other as resources and accept the responsibility of managing tasks.

Team members must also study assigned material individually to ensure their preparation for classes. There are individual assessment tests to measure if students have not only read the assigned material, but also understand the concepts of the module, and can apply them to given problems. Additional team assessment tests present a problem for discussion and require consensus, helping students learn critical communication skills. This also enables them to deal with conflicts between members before they escalate to crises. Team presentations (written or verbal)

allow the team to focus and build cohesion, with team members sharing the responsibility for presenting and persuading the audience to accept their viewpoint. Feedback on how the team is functioning with task management, team dynamics and overall work is given by the facilitator. Team exercises that are application-oriented help students experience the practical application of concepts and learn from other students' perspectives.

Team-based classrooms are especially beneficial in colleges with international students. Since this type of learning encourages people to listen and communicate with others, share problems, resolve personal conflicts, and manage their time and resources, it is a great environment for students who are in a new social situation. Since social interaction plays an important role during teamwork, team learning has an added advantage for students who are not comfortable in traditional classroom settings. It allows students from different cultures to understand their differences and use them productively. This type of learning environment also allows students to express themselves freely in a team context, rather than feeling singled out as when answering questions in a traditional classroom.

This learning model was designed to better prepare students for today's global workplace. Students are encouraged to explore ideas together, to build communication skills and achieve superior results. It is likely that employers will increasingly seek out students with these skills as we move into the future.

Questions 26–40

Questions 26–32

Complete the summary below. Choose your answers from the box below the summary.
There are more words than you will need to fill the gaps.

EXAMPLE	
	Answer
Although IT is one of the leading career	*choices*

Although IT is one of the leading career ...*(Example)*... made by graduates today, the industry's

demand for qualified applicants **[26]** .... the supply of skilled IT personnel.

Despite the **[27]** .... widespread use of computer technology in all areas of life,

[28] .... face difficulties recruiting people whose education has equipped them

to commence working productively without further training. Several business organisations

now offer income and other **[29]** .... inducements to potential employees.

They also include group **[30]** .... in their selection procedures, often inviting up

to forty **[31]** .... to their company for the two-day visit. In this way the

company can demonstrate the reality of the working **[32]** .... which is more

likely to involve challenging co-operative projects than individualised tasks.

List of Words

exceeds	extracts	choices	candidates	employees
admiration	previous	financial	employment	regularity
advantages	employers	environment	activities	current

Questions 33–37

Do the following statements reflect the views of the writer of the passage?

Write:

YES	*if the statement reflects the views of the writer.*
NO	*if the statement contradicts the writer.*
NOT GIVEN	*if it is impossible to say what the writer thinks about this.*

[33] The American Intercontinental University includes team-based learning in all its courses on all its campuses.

[34] The composition of teams is changed regularly.

[35] Theoretical problems are the most important team activity.

[36] The team members participate in assessment of other team members.

[37] International students prefer traditional classroom learning to team-based learning.

Questions 38–40

Choose one phrase from the list of phrases **A–H** below to complete each of the following sentences. There are more phrases than questions so you will not use all of them.

[38] Students' work is assessed...

[39] The teams make a joint presentation...

[40] The need to achieve consensus assists ....

List of Phrases

A	to compete with other teams as judged by the facilitator.
B	by individual tests and exams.
C	to see who has the strongest point of view in the group.
D	individually, by their peers and as a team.
E	in the development of communication skills.
F	to practise working as a group while putting theory into practice.
G	to assist international and non-traditional students.
H	in getting to know new friends and colleagues.

Passage 1

You should spend about 20 minutes on Questions 1–13 which are based on this passage.

Sleeping on the job

North Americans are not a people of the siesta. There is a tendency to associate afternoon naps with laziness and non-productivity. Latin Americans and some in European cultures take a different view. In Mexico and Greece, for example, it is customary to close businesses between noon and about 4.00 pm – siesta time. Recent studies are showing that if you can take a 15 to 30-minute nap while at work in the afternoon, you'll be more alert, more energetic, happier doing what you do, more productive and therefore more likely to get ahead. Napping on the job is not yet a trend but there is serious talk in academic circles about the merits of 'power napping'.

By some estimates, the average American collects an annual 'sleep debt' of 500 hours – subtracting from an assumed norm of eight hours a night. Two out of three Americans get less than eight hours of sleep a night during the work week, according to a recent study by the National Sleep Foundation in Washington. Forty percent say they're so tired that it interferes with their daily activities. Sleep researcher William Anthony, a professor of psychology at Boston University, says fatigue is a significant problem in modern society. He says sleepiness is a leading cause of auto accidents, second only to drunkenness. All that drowsiness costs an estimated $18 billion annually in lost productivity. 'We have a simple message,' says Professor Anthony. 'People should be allowed to nap at their breaks. The rationale is a productivity one – workers are sleepy, and when they're sleepy on the job they're not productive.'

Some companies are encouraging sleep at work, primarily for safety. The Metropolitan Transit Authority, which runs the New York subway system and two suburban railroads, is considering power naps for its train operators and bus drivers. Another railway has started letting its train operators take nap breaks of up to 45 minutes but only when trains are stopped at designated spots off the main lines and dispatchers have been notified. Some overseas air carriers permit airline pilots, when not on duty, to nap in the cockpit. Airlines in the United States have not accepted this practice yet.

According to the Encyclopedia of Sleep and Dreaming: 'There is a biologically-based tendency to fall asleep in mid-afternoon just as there is a tendency to fall asleep at night. Moreover, if sleep the night before is reduced or disturbed for any reason, a nap the subsequent afternoon is not only more likely to occur, but it can also relieve sleepiness and increase alertness.' The nap zone, documented in numerous studies, is typically between noon and 3.00 pm. Some people power through this natural slowdown with caffeine or sugar but if employers allowed naps, the benefits would be improvements in mood and performance, especially in mid-afternoon. Workers would concentrate better and persevere in tasks longer. Workers commonly sneak naps even without permission but some companies have begun encouraging naps as part of their policies on boosting production. One US distributor, is opening a 2,000-square-foot nap facility that provides beds for up to 20 of its 225 workers at a time. A company in Japan sets up tents in business offices, provides eyeshades and ear plugs and encourages employees to snooze in the middle of the work day. According to Professor Anthony, 'You're not going to see napping at traditional types of operations..... but in 21st century-style operations, this isn't going to be a perk. It's going to have more to do with productivity. Smart employers are understanding that their employees need rest to do their best.'

Some suspect that corporate naptime, like other perks, is just a way to keep people at the office longer. On the other hand, growing flexibility in hours, for some workers is allowing nap times to become more common. With eleven million Americans telecommuting and another forty million working out of their homes full- or part-time, office hours are basically as long as you can stay awake. One thing is sure: longer commutes, more intense, stressful workdays and higher production demands are taking a toll. So, with Americans sleeping less and working longer hours, some employers are warming up to the idea that a little nap in the middle of the day can be good for business.

Questions 1–13

Question 1
*Circle the correct answer **A–D**.*

[1] According to the passage, which of the following statements is supported by recent research?

    A   Napping is an indicator of laziness.
    B   Two thirds of Americans sleep too much.
    C   Napping in the workplace is a current trend.
    D   Short naps at work increase productivity.

Questions 2–6
Do the following statements reflect the claims of the writer in Passage 1?

Write:

YES	*if the statement reflects the claims of the writer.*
NO	*if the statement contradicts the writer.*
NOT GIVEN	*if it is impossible to say what the writer thinks about this.*

[2] The number one cause of car accidents is fatigue.

[3] People who nap in the afternoon are lazy.

[4] A nap in the middle of the day can improve your mood.

[5] People who nap regularly live longer.

[6] The majority of Americans sleep at least eight hours a night.

Questions 7–9
*Choose one phrase from the list in the box **(A–F)** to complete each of the following sentences.*

[7] Humans are biologically programmed to ...

[8] Employees of some progressive companies are encouraged to...

[9] Traditional employers are likely to...

A	drink coffee to stay awake during the afternoon
B	have a nap during breaks
C	fall asleep when they are bored
D	sneak naps without permission
E	resist the trend toward napping
F	fall asleep in the afternoon

Questions 10–11

Complete the following sentences using **NO MORE THAN THREE WORDS FROM THE PASSAGE.**

[10] In the transportation industry napping is a matter of... ~~priority~~ for safety.

[11] On some airlines pilots can sleep in the cockpit if... not on duty

Questions 12–13

Circle the correct answer **A–D.**

[12] According to the writer, in America the workplace is becoming...

A less flexible.
B more exciting.
C less demanding.
D more stressful.

[13] According to the writer, what is the main reason why employers support the idea of naps at work?

A for health reasons
B to promote safety
C to increase productivity
D to encourage creativity

Passage 2

You should spend about 20 minutes on Questions 14–26 which are based on this passage.

Homeopathy

A Homeopathy is an alternative system of medicine, founded in the early 19th century by a German physician, Dr. Samuel Hahnemann. Since 1980 homeopathy has experienced a strong resurgence of interest in North and South America as well as in Europe. Surveys indicate that more than a third of French physicians have prescribed homeopathic remedies and almost 50 per cent of British physicians have referred patients for homeopathic treatment.

B Hahnemann's discovery of the principle of homeopathy was accidental. After taking some quinine he noticed that he developed malaria-like symptoms. Since malaria patients were treated with quinine, he speculated that possibly malaria is cured by quinine because it causes malaria-like symptoms in healthy people. He decided to explore his theory by testing other substances used as medicine at the time, such as arsenic and belladonna. His tests were conducted by either taking the substances internally himself or by administering them to healthy volunteers and then recording all of the symptoms the volunteers experienced. He continued his experiments on a wide range of natural substances, often toxic. These recorded results created 'drug pictures' which formed the basis for the new system of medicine. The next step was to give the tested substances to patients suffering from the same group of symptoms represented by the drug picture recorded. The results were incredible. People were being cured from diseases that had never been cured before. He condensed his theory into a single Latin phrase: *similia similibus curentur* (let likes be cured by likes). This means that a disease can be cured by a medicine which produces in a healthy person, symptoms similar to those experienced by the patient.

C The process of making remedies is very precise. A homeopathic remedy is normally a single substance. The substances may be made from plants, minerals and even animals, for example snake venom and cuttlefish ink. To make remedies, the raw material is dissolved in a mixture that contains approximately 90% alcohol and 10 % water. The mixture is left to stand for 2 to 4 weeks, shaken occasionally then strained. The resulting liquid or tincture is then diluted according to very specific measures to a factor of 1:100. For example, to produce a remedy called 1c potency or strength, one drop of the tincture is added to 99 drops of alcohol/water mixture. To produce a 2c potency one drop of the 1c mixture is added to 99 drops of alcohol/water mixture. Between each mixture the remedy is shaken vigorously. Hahnemann believed that through this process, the energy of the substance was released. Once the remedy has been diluted beyond a 12c potency it is unlikely that even a molecule of the original substance remains. Yet, ironically, the more dilute the remedy, the stronger it is. This makes no sense in light of present day science but regardless of what science tells us is impossible, in practice, the higher the dilution the stronger and more lasting the effect.

D It is this use of high dilutions that has given rise to controversy. Many conventional doctors claim that homeopathy functions only as a placebo because the dosage is so small. However, the clinical experience of homeopathy shows that this tiny dose can be effective: it works on unconscious people and infants, and it even works on animals. Controlled clinical studies performed by medical researchers are demonstrating that homeopathy can be an effective method of treatment for many diseases.

E The most important part of homeopathic treatment lies in the lengthy interview which the homeopath conducts with the patient. The idea behind this one to two hour consultation is to build up a psychological, emotional and physical history of the patient, to discover the underlying patterns of disease. The homeopath then decides which medicine to prescribe based on the closest match between the patient's symptoms and the known symptoms elicited by the medicine in a healthy body. A single dose is given for the shortest period of time necessary to stimulate the body's healing power.

F How does the concept of homeopathy differ from that of conventional medicine? Very simply, homeopathy attempts to stimulate the body to recover itself. Instead of looking upon the symptoms as something wrong which must be set right, the homeopath sees them as signs of the way the body is attempting to help itself. Another basic difference between conventional medical therapy and homeopathy is in the role of medication. In much of conventional therapy the illness is controlled through regular use of medical substances. If the medication is withdrawn, the person returns to illness. For example, a person who takes a pill for high blood pressure every day is not undergoing a cure but is only controlling the symptoms. Homeopathy's aim is the cure: 'The complete restoration of perfect health,' as Dr. Hahnemann said.

G Homeopathy has made significant progress in treating diseases which orthodox medicine finds difficult. Best at dealing with inflammatory conditions such as arthritis, skin conditions, migraines and respiratory problems linked to allergies, it has also proved highly successful at treating asthma. But homeopathy is not an appropriate treatment for degenerative diseases such as emphysema. It cannot treat diseases which destroy tissue, although it can still be beneficial if used in combination with other treatments. Two of the main advantages of homeotherapy are the low cost of the medications and the rarity of adverse reactions. The medicines are inexpensive, safe, and easy to use, so people can learn to handle many of the common illnesses for which they currently seek medical help. The resulting savings in costs and the increase in personal independence represent a significant contribution to health care.

Questions 14–26

Questions 14–19

The reading passage has 7 sections A–G.

Choose the most suitable headings for sections B–G from the list of headings (i–x). There are more headings than sections so you will not use all of them.

List of Headings

(i)	The future of homeopathy
(ii)	Concerns about homeopathy
(iii)	Comparison with traditional western medicine
(iv)	Dr. S. Hahnemann
(v)	Theoretical and experimental basis
(vi)	Revival of homeopathy
(vii)	Preparation of medicines
(viii)	Debate over effectiveness
(ix)	Advantages and limitations of homeopathy
(x)	Aspects of treatment

EXAMPLE		Answer
	Section **A**	*vi*

[14]	Section **B**	
[15]	Section **C**	
[16]	Section **D**	
[17]	Section **E**	
[18]	Section **F**	
[19]	Section **G**	

Questions 20–22

Complete the description below. Choose *NO MORE THAN THREE WORDS FROM THE PASSAGE* for each answer.

Making a homeopathic remedy

The remedies come from plant, animal and mineral sources.

A single product is mixed with **[20]** .... and left to stand for 2–4 weeks.

This mixture is strained to produce a tincture which can be diluted.

1 drop of this tincture is added to 99 drops of alcohol/water.

The mixture is then **[21]** .... vigorously.

This produces a remedy with a potency of 1c.

As the remedy becomes more diluted it gets **[22]** ....

Questions 23–26

Complete the summary. Choose your answers from the box below.

Homeopathy differs from conventional medicine in a number of ways. Conventional medicine views symptoms as an indication of something wrong in the body whereas homeopathy sees them as signs that the body is attempting to **[23]** .... The uses of medication differ also. Many types of conventional medication **[24]** .... but if the medicine is taken away, the illness returns. The intention of homeopathy is to bring about a complete cure. Homeopathic remedies are **[25]** .... than conventional medicine and have fewer **[26]** ....

List of words/phrases

cheaper	cure	heal itself
illness	treatments	getting better
control symptoms	more expensive	side effects
stronger	healthy	patients

You should spend about 20 minutes on Questions 27–40 which are based on this passage.

The hemp revival

The hemp plant, one of the world's oldest industrial resources, is back. The rediscovery of this renewable resource is making it the fibre of choice for future textiles, personal care products, building materials, paper and fuel.

Hemp has been grown for paper, textiles, food and medicine throughout human history. The earliest known woven fabric, made of hemp, dates back to the eighth millennium (8,000–7,000 BC). The majority of all sails, clothes, tents, rugs, towels, paper, rope, twine, art canvas, paints, varnishes and lighting oil were made from hemp. Hemp seeds were regularly used as a source of food and protein for centuries.

Hemp's drastic decline in use and importance within a matter of fifty years is widely considered to have been brought about by the timber and petrochemical industries in America. By the mid-1930s, changes in technology were beginning to impact on the hemp industry. Mechanical stripping equipment and machines to conserve hemp's high-cellulose pulp became available and affordable. Timber and paper holding companies stood to lose billions of dollars if hemp were to be grown on a large scale. A resurgence of the hemp industry also threatened the emerging petro-chemical companies which had patented the chemicals for pulp processing. Newspaper articles began to appear, linking hemp with violent crime. The term used, however, was 'marijuana' to distance it from hemp used for industrial purposes. Because few people realised that marijuana and hemp came from the same plant species, virtually nobody suspected that the Marijuana Prohibition of 1938 would destroy the hemp industry.

Supporting the theory that marijuana was banned to destroy the hemp industry, were two articles written just before the Marijuana Prohibition, claiming that hemp was on the verge of becoming a super crop. These articles, which appeared in well-respected magazines, praised the usefulness and potential of hemp. 'Hemp can be used to produce more than 25,000 products', and 'hemp will prove, for both farmer and public, the most profitable and desirable crop that can be grown.' This was the first time that 'billion dollar' was used to describe the value of a crop. Less than one year after these articles were written the Marijuana Prohibition took effect. To what extent a conspiracy was involved is still being debated, but the important thing is that for thousands of years, hemp was used extensively. Then over a short period, it became illegal in many parts of the world.

Now, however, the focus is on the development of hemp as an industrial resource. Initially, a distinction needs to be made between the two types of hemp. 'Cannabis has evolved into two basic species. Plants grown for fibre and seed are universally called hemp. Cannabis grown for its drug content is commonly called marijuana or drug cannabis. Drug-type cannabis varies widely in THC content from approximately 1–2% in unselected strains to 10% in the best modern varieties.' (as cited from Watson 1994). Hemp contains virtually none of the active ingredients of drug-type cannabis (THC). It is not feasible to 'get high' on hemp, and most marijuana produces very low-quality fibre. Hemp should never be confused with marijuana, as their roles can not be reversed.

It is evident that hemp is an extraordinary fibre. Both stems and seeds can be utilised. Most significantly, hemp can be grown without pesticides and herbicides. The plant also has the ability to suppress weeds and soil-borne diseases. Based on the hemp industries which have been established overseas, there is a large demand for hemp products and hemp is proving to be a highly profitable industry. On an annual basis, one acre of hemp will produce as much fibre as 2 to 3 acres of cotton. The fibre is stronger and softer than cotton, lasts twice as long and will not mildew. Cotton grows only in warm climates and requires more water and more fertiliser than hemp as well as large quantities of pesticide and herbicide.

Hemp can also be used to produce fibreboard that is stronger and lighter than wood, and is fire retardant. Unlike paper from wood pulp, hemp paper contains no dioxin, or other toxic residue, and a single acre of hemp can produce the same amount of paper as four acres of trees. The trees take 20 years to harvest and hemp takes a single season. In warm climates hemp can be harvested two or even three times a year. On an annual basis, one acre of hemp will produce as much paper as 2 to 4 acres of trees. From tissue paper to cardboard, all types of paper products can be produced from hemp. The quality of hemp paper is superior to tree-based paper. Hemp paper will last hundreds of years without degrading and it can be recycled many more times than tree-based paper.

Today, industrialised nations around the world are waking up to the enormous potential of hemp. While some countries, like China and India, have never had laws against hemp cultivation, others are legalising industrial hemp after many years of lumping it together with marijuana. The products and fabrics that are emerging from the international hemp industry are finding strong demand in an eco-aware global community. Hemp is indeed an agricultural crop for the twenty-first century.

Questions 27–40

Questions 27–31

Re-order the following letters (A-F) to show the sequence of events according to the passage. The first one has been done for you as an example.

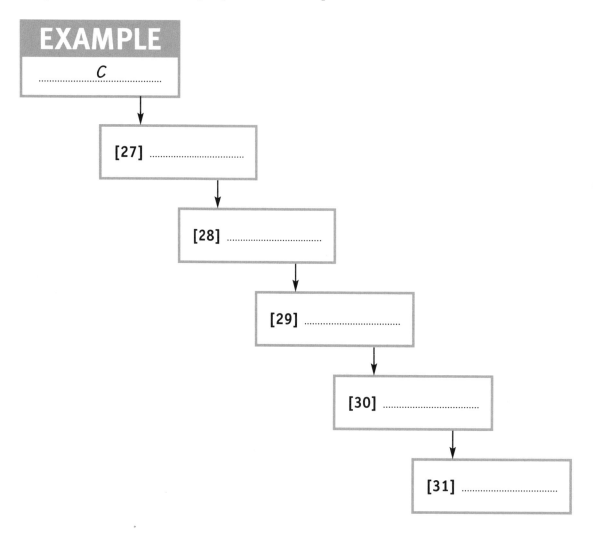

EXAMPLE

.... *C* ....

→ [27] ....

→ [28] ....

→ [29] ....

→ [30] ....

→ [31] ....

A	Timber and petro-chemical industries threatened	
B	Articles praise hemp as a potential billion dollar crop	
C	Widespread cultivation of hemp	*Example*
D	Prohibition of marijuana	
E	Newspaper articles link hemp to violent crime	
F	Development of stripping machines	

Questions 32–33

Complete the following using **NO MORE THAN THREE WORDS FROM THE PASSAGE.**

	Hemp	Marijuana
Fibre	strong and durable	[32] ....
Drug Content	[33]	up to 10%THC

Questions 34–39

From the information given in the passage, classify the following **(34–39)** as characteristic of:

- **A** Hemp
- **B** Wood
- **C** Cotton

[34]   mildew-resistant

[35]   dioxin is a by-product of processing

[36]   can be harvested more than once a year

[37]   large amounts of fertiliser needed

[38]   fire-retardant properties

[39]   requires mild temperature

Question 40

Choose the correct answer **A–D**.

[40] The main purpose of this article is...

- **A**   to criticise government policy on hemp.
- **B**   to show the economic benefits of hemp.
- **C**   to compare hemp and marijuana.
- **D**   to promote research into new uses of hemp.

Passage 1

You should spend about 20 minutes on Questions 1–13 which are based on this passage.

Frogwatch

Frogwatch, a remarkable success story started in Western Australia, is the brainchild of Dr Ken Aplin. His work as the curator of reptiles and frogs in the Western Australian Museum, involved long field trips and he wondered if a community-based frog-monitoring network could help him keep track of frogs. Through such a network, ordinary untrained members of the community could learn about frog habitats, observe the numbers and kinds of frogs in their local area, and report this information to the museum.

Launched in 1995, Frogwatch recently gained its 3221st member, and many people say that this is the best thing the museum has ever done. Each participant receives a 'Frogwatch Kit' – a regular newsletter, an audio tape of frog calls and identification sheets. Recently, Frogwatch membership increased dramatically when a mysterious parasitic fungus disease began attacking frogs nationwide. Although research is yet incomplete, scientists suspect the fungus originated overseas, perhaps in South America, where frogs have died in catastrophic numbers from a fungus disease genetically similar to the Australian organism.

Researchers in Western Australia needed to know how widespread the infection was in the state's frog populations. So Aplin sent an 'F-file' (frog fungus facts) alert to Frogwatch members, requesting their help. He asked them to deliver him dead or dying frogs. More than 2000 frogs have now been examined, half from the museum's existing collection. Aplin once thought the fungus had arrived in Western Australia in only the past year or two, but tests now suggest it has been there since the late 1980s.

Frogwatch has proved to be the perfect link to the public and Aplin has become a total convert to community participation. He's now aiming for a network of 15,000 Frogwatch members as the museum can't afford to use professional resources to monitor frog populations. Much of the frog habitat is on private land, and without community support, monitoring the frogs would be impossible.

Not everyone is convinced by the 'feelgood' popularity of Frogwatch. While Aplin believes even tiny backyard ponds can help to significantly improve frog numbers, Dr Dale Roberts isn't so sure. A senior zoology lecturer at the University of WA, Roberts agrees the program has tapped into the public's enthusiasm for frogs, but he warns that strong public awareness does not amount to sound science.

He argues that getting the public to send in pages of observations is a good thing, but giving these reports credibility may not be valid scientifically. In addition he's not convinced that Frogwatch's alarmist message about the danger of fungal infection is valid either. In Western Australia, for example, there was a long summer and very late drenching rains that year, following two equally dry years. So, he argues, there are other things that might have precipitated the deaths. He questions what could be done about it anyway. If it's already widespread, it may not be worth the cost and effort of doing anything about it. Even if it's causing high death rates, he says he can still find every frog species found over the past ten years in the south-west of Australia.

Roberts argues that Western Australia is different. Unlike most other states, species are still being discovered there; the disappearances of frog types in Queensland and New South Wales, are not occurring in Western Australia, although three south-west species are on the endangered list. Roberts believes that no amount of garden ponds in Perth will help those species, which live in isolated habitats targeted for development.

Aplin's response is that increasing the number of frog-friendly habitats is important for the very reason that many West Australian frog species are found in small, highly restricted locations. He argues that pesticide-free gardens and ponds can offer a greater chance of survival to animals battling habitat disturbance, environmental pollutants, climatic variations, and now fungal disease. Aplin's opinion is that they should use the precautionary principle in cases where they don't yet know enough about the situation. Usually diseases sort themselves out naturally and some frog fauna will co-evolve with the fungus. Given time some balance may be restored, but in the shorter term, they are seeing negative impacts.

The nationwide spread of the chytrid fungus is being mapped by Dr Rick Speare, a specialist in amphibian disease at James Cook University. Speare also tests the accuracy of Aplin's fungus diagnoses and says Frogwatch is 'an amazing and under-acknowledged system...the best program in Australia for harnessing public interest in frog biology...There are a lot of eyes out there looking for dead or sick frogs, beyond the power of any biologist to collect.'

Aplin argues that they should never underestimate the importance of having a community base, especially when governments want to cut research funds. 'People can protest in ways that a handful of scientists hiding in a laboratory can't do. For just about every environmental problem, community involvement is fundamental'. Furthermore Frogwatch is proving to be a social phenomenon as much as anything else. It seems ordinary people know that frogs are a measure of the environment's health.

Questions 1–13

Questions 1–6

Do the following statements reflect the claims of the writer of the passage?

Write:

YES	*if the statement reflects the claims of the writer.*
NO	*if the statement contradicts the claims of the writer.*
NOT GIVEN	*if it is impossible to say what the writer thinks about this.*

[1]   Frogwatch members need a basic level of scientific training.

[2]   All Frogwatch members live in Western Australia.

[3]   Frogwatch has proved that frogs are disappearing because of a fungus.

[4]   Scientists in WA have examined about two thousand frogs collected by Frogwatch.

[5]   The frog fungus disease has been in Western Australia for more than ten years.

[6]   New species of frogs have been found in Western Australia recently.

Questions 7–12

*The reading passage describes the opinions of **Dr Ken Aplin**, **Dr Dale Roberts** and **Dr Rick Speare** in relation to strategies for frog conservation.*

*Match one of the researchers **A–C** to each of the statements below.*
There may be more than one correct answer.

Write:

        A for Dr Aplin
        B for Dr Roberts
        C for Dr Speare

[7] Although the involvement of large numbers of people is encouraging, this does not guarantee scientifically valid data.

[8] The development of frog-friendly backyards will help to conserve frog species.

[9] Although it is possible that frogs will adapt to fungal and other problems in the long term, we should take precautions in case this does not occur.

[10] As there may be many other explanations for recent frog deaths, it is not worth spending a great deal of time and money studying this fungus.

[11] Because of the unique geography of Western Australia most frog species in this State are not in danger of extinction.

[12] Frogwatch has greater potential for frog observation than is possible by the scientific community.

Question 13
Write the appropriate letter A–D.

[13] The main purpose of Frogwatch is...

A   for people to collect and deliver dead or dying frogs to scientists.
B   for people to observe and collect information about frog populations for scientists.
C   for people to allow scientists onto their private land to look at frog habitats.
D   for people to set up ponds in their gardens as habitat for frogs.

Passage 2

You should spend about 20 minutes on Questions 14–28 which are based on this passage.

Just relax......

A Hypnosis is an intriguing and fascinating process. A trance-like mental state is induced in one person by another, who appears to have the power to command that person to obey instructions without question. Hypnotic experiences were described by the ancient Egyptians and Greeks, whilst references to deep sleep and anaesthesia have been found in the Bible and in the Jewish Talmud. In the mid-1700s, Franz Mesmer, an Austrian physician, developed his theory of 'animal magnestism', which was the belief that the cause of disease was the 'improper distribution of invisible magnetic fluids'. Mesmer used water tubs and magnetic wands to direct these supposed fluids to his patients. In 1784, a French commission studied Mesmer's claims, and concluded that these 'cures' were only imagined by the patients. However, people continued to believe in this process of 'mesmerism' and it was soon realised that successful results could be achieved, but without the need for magnets and water.

B The term *hypnotism* was first used by James Braid, a British physician who studied suggestion and hypnosis in the mid-1800s. He demonstrated that hypnosis differed from sleep, that it was a physiological response and not the result of secret powers. During this same period, James Esdaile, a Scottish doctor working in India, used hypnotism instead of anaesthetic in over 200 major surgical operations, including leg amputations. Later that century, a French neurologist, Jean Charcot, successfully experimented with hypnosis in his clinic for nervous disorders.

C Since then, scientists have shown that the state of hypnosis is a natural human behaviour, which can affect psychological, social and/or physical experiences. The effects of hypnotism depend on the ability, willingness and motivation of the person being hypnotised. Although hypnosis has been compared to dreaming and sleepwalking, it is not actually related to sleep. It involves a more active and intense mental concentration of the person being hypnotised. Hypnotised people can talk, write, and walk about and they are usually fully aware of what is being said and done.

D There are various techniques used to induce hypnosis. The best-known is a series of simple suggestions repeated continuously in the same tone of voice. The subject is instructed to focus their attention on an object or fixed point, while being told to relax, breathe deeply, and allow the eyelids to grow heavy and close. As the person responds, their state of attention changes, and this altered state often leads to other changes. For example, the person may experience different levels of awareness, consciousness, imagination, memory and reasoning or become more responsive to suggestions. Additional phenomena may be produced or eliminated such as blushing, sweating, paralysis, muscle tension or anaesthesia. Although these changes can occur with hypnosis, none of these experiences is unique to it. People who are very responsive to hypnosis are also more responsive to suggestions when they are not hypnotised. This responsiveness increases during hypnotism. This explains why hypnosis takes only a few seconds for some, whilst other people cannot be easily hypnotised.

E It is a common misunderstanding that hypnotists are able to force people to perform criminal or any other acts against their will. In fact, subjects can resist suggestions, and they retain their ability to distinguish right from wrong. This misunderstanding is often the result of public performances where subjects perform ridiculous or highly embarrassing actions at the command of the hypnotist. These people are usually instructed not to recall their behaviour after re-emerging from the hypnotic state, so it appears that they were powerless while hypnotised. The point to remember however, is that these individuals chose to participate, and the success of hypnotism depends on the willingness of a person to be hypnotised.

F Interestingly, there are different levels of hypnosis achievable. Thus deep hypnosis can be induced to allow anaesthesia for surgery, childbirth or dentistry. This contrasts to a lighter state of hypnosis, which deeply relaxes the patient who will then follow simple directions. This latter state may be used to treat mental health problems, as it allows patients to feel calm while simultaneously thinking about distressing feelings or painful memories. Thus patients can learn new responses to situations or come up with solutions to problems. This can help recovery from psychological conditions such as anxiety, depression or phobias. Sometimes, after traumatic incidents, memory of the events may be blocked. For example, some soldiers develop amnesia [loss of memory] as a result of their experiences during wartime. Through hypnosis these repressed memories can be retrieved and treated. A variation of this treatment involves age regression, when the hypnotist takes the patient back to a specific age. In this way patients may remember events and feelings from that time, which may be affecting their current wellbeing.

G Physicians also have made use of the ability of a hypnotised person to remain in a given position for long periods of time. In one case, doctors had to graft skin onto a patient's badly damaged foot. First, skin from the person's abdomen was grafted onto his arm; then the graft was transferred to his foot. With hypnosis, the patient held his arm tightly in position over his abdomen for three weeks, then over his foot for four weeks. Even though these positions were unusual, the patient at no time felt uncomfortable!

H Hypnosis occasionally has been used with witnesses and victims of crime to enable people to remember important clues, such as a criminal's physical appearance or other significant details that might help to solve a crime. However, as people can both lie and make mistakes while hypnotised, the use of hypnotism in legal situations can cause serious problems. Also hypnosis cannot make a person divulge secret information if they don't want to. This was confirmed by the Council on Scientific Affairs of the American Medical Association, which in 1985 reported that memories refreshed through hypnosis may include inaccurate information, false memories, and confabulation (fact and fantasy combined).

Questions 14–28

Questions 14–18

*The passage has eight sections **A–H**. Choose the most suitable heading for sections **B–F** from the list of headings below. Write the appropriate numbers **(i–x)**.*

There are more headings than sections, so you will not use all of them.

EXAMPLE	Answer
Section **A**	**(x)**

[14] Section **B**

[15] Section **C**

[16] Section **D**

[17] Section **E**

[18] Section **F**

List of Headings

(i)   Use of hypnotism in criminal cases
(ii)   The normality of hypnotised subjects' behaviour
(iii)   Early medical experiments with hypnotism
(iv)   Early association of hypnosis with psychology
(v)   Dangers of hypnotism
(vi)   How to hypnotise
(vii)   Hypnosis and free will
(viii) Difference between mesmerism and hypnotism
(ix)   Therapeutic uses of hypnosis
(x)   Origins of hypnosis   **EXAMPLE**

Questions 19–23

*Complete the notes on the history of hypnosis using **NO MORE THAN THREE WORDS FROM THE PASSAGE**.*

References to hypnotism can be found in both the Talmud and the **[19]** .... Even

when Mesmer's **[20]** .... were not used, successful results occurred without them.

Braid identified hypnosis as a natural **[21]** .... response, rather than magical or

mystical. Early psychological studies showed the difference between sleep and hypnosis.

Successful hypnosis requires the subject's active **[22]** .... Consequently subjects

can speak or move around and are **[23]** .... of their surroundings.

Questions 24–28

Choose the correct letter **A–D**.

[24] In order to induce hypnosis the hypnotist will...

- **A** encourage the person to relax using a repetitively even tone of voice.
- **B** say a specific set of words in a special tone of voice.
- **C** say any words but in a particular tone of voice.
- **D** encourage the person to relax while focussing on a slowly moving object.

[25] Hypnotised subjects can be instructed to...

- **A** do something they have previously said is against their wishes.
- **B** demonstrate physical strength they would normally not have.
- **C** reveal confidential information against their will.
- **D** do something that they would not normally be opposed to doing.

[26] Past events are recalled under hypnosis...

- **A** to entertain the hypnotist.
- **B** to allow subjects to reassess them without distress.
- **C** to help the subjects improve their memories.
- **D** to make the subject feel younger.

[27] After surgery, hypnosis may be used...

- **A** to make drugs unnecessary.
- **B** to keep the patient mobile.
- **C** to make the patient forget to move.
- **D** to minimise patient's discomfort while immobile.

[28] The American Medical Association reported that...

- **A** people lie when giving evidence under hypnosis.
- **B** people should be hypnotised before giving evidence.
- **C** evidence given when hypnotised may be unreliable.
- **D** secret evidence can be obtained through hypnosis.

Passage 3

You should spend about 20 minutes on Questions 29–40 which are based on this passage.

KIDSAND

Two Italian psychologists, Vincenzo Marte and Giovanni Notarnicola, describe the traditional spontaneous practice of sport by children – climbing trees, riding a bicycle along quiet roads, racing their friends across the fields – as an activity of *freedom,* a special activity of discovery and learning. In the case of *free* sporting activity, the child's time is given up entirely to the activity, as can be seen in the endless games of football young children play, which may then be followed by bicycle races and/or a swim in the river, for example.

Today, however, children's discovery of sport has become very different. It is often parents who take their children, when they are very young, to the swimming pool or to the sports grounds or sports halls. Children's first experience of sport thus takes place as an organised activity, which they see as organisation of their free time. By organising sport for children, and often deciding for them, we unfortunately create an imbalance preventing them from managing their own play/sports time, thus denying them an opportunity of autonomy and independence as was possible in the past.

A first possible reason for the imbalance in the practice of sport by children is therefore linked to the urban society we live in today. We need not regret the past; it

is rather a question of knowing how to recreate this freedom in our towns and in the country, where sport is increasingly based on organised leisure activities. Doing one sport is now the rule in clubs. Sports grounds are often on the outskirts of cities, and are overcrowded and invariably enclosed, while recreational areas such as parks or hard-packed surfaces, are very few and far between. How can we find the balance of a varied and spontaneous relationship to sport under such conditions?

Some interesting answers have already been suggested which take into account the need to recreate this freedom. Marte and Notarnicola have shown that children who have experienced such freedom were considered by sports trainers to be more capable when they joined organised sport aged 12–13. Their study concluded that no formal training, no matter how early in life it took place, could replace these first experiences.

Measures which would reverse this imbalance include: increasing the number of sports facilities which encourage self-organisation by the children, and also setting up unstructured playing areas with little in the way of equipment. Areas where street sport can be practised need to be established and sports clubs which offer multidisciplinary sports training should be supported. Children should be offered pre-school activity where they can the discover different sports.

For children, sport remains a special kind of discovery and learning, no matter how much adults limit and control the practice of early intensive training. Here is the second example of imbalance in children's sport. Today, sport is practised with early intensive training from the youngest possible age. Sometimes this is even before the age of six and is usually one specific sport within an organised framework. When adult-style competitions are introduced at an early age, the conditions which encourage a balanced development of children through sport are no longer respected.

Today, early intensive training is much more widely on offer. Many sports organisations claim that they are forced to do to this type of training because of what is called 'the golden age' to acquire the physical skills. It is considered unthinkable for a young skater or gymnast to miss this period, because if they did so, they would fall so far behind the best, that they could never hope to catch up. Faced with this demand for early ability, it is important that a safety net is put in place to maximise the benefits and minimise the disadvantages of such intensive training.

Why do very young children give up sport? The most common reason for leaving a sport is to change to another sport, which in itself is no bad thing. However, children may leave a sport because they believe that they have received too much criticism and too many negative assessments. We know that young children, up to the age of eleven or twelve, cannot assess their own level of competence. They believe that if they are making an effort, then this in itself is a sign of their competence. We also know that young children are particularly sensitive to criticism from adults or peers. Trainers must therefore pay particular attention to this and avoid excessive criticism. They should also avoid

any strategies that discriminate against the child: for example in team sports, naming first choice players and reserves. It should be remembered that primary school children's main desire is to have fun and socialise. The desire to improve and become a good competitor will develop later. This brief example shows that knowledge of child development is indispensable for those who take care of children at this age. It is up to trainers, sports doctors and psychologists to implement the measures necessary to limit this excessive early practice of sport by children.

A third source of imbalance which threatens children and sport is parental attitudes. The American psychologist, Rainer Martens, emphasises that, 'too often children's joy of sports is destroyed by adults who want glory through victory.' Several studies have shown that parental pressure is high on the list of reasons why children leave sport. The presence of mothers and fathers can prevent children from considering sport as their own, where they can learn to master technical difficulties, manage interpersonal relations, and experience success and failure. As Martens highlights, 'adults are solely to blame if joy and sadness become synonymous, to a child, with victory or defeat.'

If the children make the decisions, this ensures that they enjoy being a child in sport, and are relaxed with their development as human beings. We need only observe the activity in a school playground, where games are organised on an improvised playing field, to understand that children show genetic traces of the hunter instinct, which naturally leads them to physical activity. Sport is included as something they want, and which they identify both as a means of release and as a form of self-expression. By acting as a route to self-discovery, sport gives children both the opportunity to know their limits, and to acquire tools which will allow them to surpass them. Playing sport is a source of learning, progress and pleasure; an additional way of enriching life.

Questions 29–40

Questions 29–36
Complete the summary below using **NO MORE THAN TWO WORDS FROM THE PASSAGE.**

Marte & Notarnicola define the spontaneous sporting games of children as activities of

[29] .... Because today sport is often decided and **[30]** .... by

parents, children lose their autonomy. A first imbalance occurs because

[31] .... are out of the city and often crowded, whilst there are a limited

number of open recreational areas where children can play spontaneously.

Children should discover and learn about sports themselves. The second imbalance occurs

because they start early **[32]** .... training very young and participate in only

[33] .... specific activity. Children often give up a sport because of negative

[34] .... It is important that trainers avoid excessive criticism of young

children, who should have **[35]** .... at sporting activities. Another reason that

children may give up sport is the attitudes of their parents. This third imbalance occurs as

parents exert **[36]** .... on children to win rather than to enjoy sport.

Questions 37–40

*Choose the correct letter **A–D**.*

[37] Children's expression of this 'freedom' is important because …

- **A** it allows them to be lazy.
- **B** it means they can learn to swim and ride a bike.
- **C** it puts them in charge of what they do and when they do it.
- **D** it relieves the parents from transporting their children to sports.

[38] Ways of allowing children to develop this 'freedom' include…

- **A** making transport to sports clubs free.
- **B** offering a range of different sports in each sports club.
- **C** offering sporting tuition to pre school children.
- **D** making children play outside regularly.

[39] To encourage young children to continue with sport we should give them…

- **A** accurate feedback about their ability at sport.
- **B** experience of failure as well as success.
- **C** experience of being reserves as well as first choice team members.
- **D** the opportunity to mix socially with their peers at sport.

[40] The author believes that…

- **A** children's sport should not be organised by adults.
- **B** playing sport is an important part of children's development.
- **C** children need to learn that sport is about losing as well as winning.
- **D** children can be psychologically and physiologically damaged by sport.

Passage 1

You should spend about 20 minutes on Questions 1–14 which are based on this passage.

WOLVES, DOGS AND HUMANS

There is no doubt that dogs are the oldest of all species tamed by humans and their domestication was based on a mutually beneficial relationship with man. The conventional view is that the domestication of wolves began between 10,000 and 20,000 years ago. However, a recent ground-breaking paper by a group of international geneticists has pushed this date back by a factor of 10. Led by Dr. Robert Wayne, at the University of California, Los Angeles, the team showed that all dog breeds had only one ancestor, the wolf. They did this by analysing the genetic history through the DNA of 162 wolves from around the world and 140 domestic dogs representing 67 breeds. The research also confirms, for the first time, that dogs are descended only from wolves and do not share DNA with coyotes or jackals. The fact that our companionship with dogs now appears to go back at least 100,000 years means that this partnership may have played an important part in the development of human hunting techniques that developed 70,000 to 90,000 years ago. It also may even have affected the brain development in both species.

The Australian veterinarian David Paxton suggests that in that period of first contact, people did not so much domesticate wolves as wolves domesticated people. Wolves may have started living at the edge of human settlements as scavengers, eating scraps of food and waste. Some learned to live with human beings in a mutually helpful way and gradually evolved into dogs. At the very least, they would have protected human settlements, and given warnings by barking at anything approaching. The wolves that evolved into dogs have been enormously successful in evolutionary terms. They are found everywhere in the inhabited world, hundreds of millions of them. The descendants of the wolves that remained wolves are now sparsely distributed, often in endangered populations.

In return for companionship and food, the early ancestor of the dog assisted humans in tracking, hunting, guarding and a variety of other activities. Eventually humans began to selectively breed these animals for specific traits. Physical characteristics changed and individual breeds began to take shape. As humans wandered across Asia and Europe, they took their dogs along, using them for additional tasks and further breeding them for selected qualities that would better enable them to perform specific duties.

According to Dr. Colin Groves, of the Department of Archaeology and Anthropology at Australian National University, early humans came to rely on dogs' keen ability to hear, smell and see – allowing certain areas of the human brain to shrink in size relative to other areas. 'Dogs acted as humans' alarm systems, trackers and hunting aids, garbage disposal facilities, hot-water bottles and children's guardians and playmates. Humans provided dogs with food and security. This symbiotic relationship was stable for over 100,000 years and intensified into mutual domestication,' said Dr. Groves. In his opinion, humans domesticated dogs and dogs domesticated humans.

Dr. Groves repeated an assertion made as early as 1914 – that humans have some of the same physical characteristics as domesticated animals, the most notable being decreased brain size. The horse experienced a 16 per cent reduction in brain size after domestication while pigs' brains shrank by as much as 34 per cent. The estimated brain-size reduction in domesticated dogs varies from 30 per cent to 10 per cent. Only in the last decade have archaeologists uncovered enough fossil evidence to establish that brain capacity in humans declined in Europe and Africa by at least 10 per cent beginning about 10,000 years ago. Dr. Groves believes this reduction may have taken place as the relationship between humans and dogs intensified. The close interaction between the two species allowed for the diminishing of certain human brain functions like smell and hearing.

Questions 1–14

Questions 1–5

Do the following statements agree with the views of the writer of the passage?

Write:

YES	*if the statement agrees with the author's views.*
NO	*if the statement contradicts the author's views.*
NOT GIVEN	*if the information is not clearly given in the passage.*

[1] The co-existence of wolves and humans began 10,000 years ago.

[2] Dogs, wolves, jackals and coyotes share a common ancestor.

[3] Wolves are a protected species in most parts of the world.

[4] Dogs evolved from wolves which chose to live with humans. Y

[5] Dogs probably influenced the development of human hunting skills. Y

Questions 6–8
*Choose the correct letter **A–D**.*

[6] How do we know that dogs have been more successful in evolutionary terms than wolves?

    A Dogs can be trained more easily than wolves.
    B Wolves are stronger than dogs.
    C Humans prefer dogs to wolves.
    D There are more dogs than wolves today.

[7] As a result of domestication, the size of the human brain has...

    A increased.
    B decreased.
    C stayed the same.
    D become more complex.

[8] What can we infer from the studies of brain size and domestication?

    A   Domestic life is less demanding than surviving in the wild.
    B   Animals like living with humans.
    C   Domestication has made animals physically weaker.
    D   Pigs are less intelligent than dogs.

Question 9

*Choose **TWO WORDS FROM THE PASSAGE** for the answer.*

There are many different types of dogs today, because, in early times humans began to

[9] ....*selectively*.................. their animals for the characteristics they wanted.
            breed

Questions 10–14

*Match one of the researchers **(A–C)** to each of the findings **(10–14)** below.*

    A   Dr. Wayne
    B   Dr. Paxton
    C   Dr. Groves

EXAMPLE	Answer
found the common ancestor of the dog	A

[10] studied the brain size of domesticated animals   *C*

[11] claims that wolves chose to interact with humans   *B*

✗ **[12]** established a new time frame for domestication of wolves   *B*

[13] believes that dogs and humans domesticated each other   *B C*

[14] studied the DNA of wolves and dogs   *A*

    13/14
    16 mks

You should spend about 20 minutes on Questions 15–28 which are based on this passage.

Crop circles

The crop circle phenomenon has puzzled and mystified humanity for many years. The designs just appear, placed carefully in fields of food grains. Some are larger than football fields and highly complex in design and construction. Others are smaller and more primitive. We call them crop circles, but many of them are not circular. Some are elongated abstract designs, a few resemble insects or other known forms, and some are mixtures of lines, circles, and other shapes melded into intricate patterns. Most become visible overnight, though it has been claimed that a few have appeared within a half-hour in broad daylight.

Crop circles have appeared all over the world. About 10,000 instances from various countries have been reported in recent years. The first modern rash of crop circles appeared in Australia in December of 1973. A strange circular imprint appeared in a wheat field near Wokurna, a community southeast of Adelaide. Soon seven swirled circles up to 14 feet in diameter appeared in an oatfield nearby. In December of 1989, an amazing set of circles, ranging from a few inches to a few feet in diameter appeared in the wheat belt west of Melbourne. As many as 90 crop circles were found. The best documented and largest modern spread of crop circles began in southern England during the summer of 1980. By the end of 1988, 112 new circles had been formed. At that time circles were being reported worldwide, 305 by the end of 1989. The total grew to an outstanding 1000 newly-formed circles in 1990. In 1991, 200 to 300 circles were reported. Crop circles have been documented in over 30 countries, including Canada, the former Soviet Union, Japan and the United States.

Nine out of ten circles remained simple with broken stems flattened to the ground and swirled. The stalks around the circles remained completely erect. But over the years, crop circles have become much more geometrically intricate. Patterns involved multiple circles, bars, triangles, rings, and spurs. Pictorial imagery also appeared. Reliable eyewitnesses have reported seeing unusual lights and hearing unidentifiable sounds while on an early-morning walk in the countryside where a crop circle showed later that day. High-pitched, warbling noises have been recorded at the site of some crop circles. On several occasions a strange glow or a darker colouring has been seen in the sky over a crop circle. And in more than one instance, the electrical power of small planes flying overhead has been cut off abruptly. While the causal energies do not seem to harm animals, or even insects as far as we can tell, wild creatures tend to avoid the circles. Flocks of birds have been seen to split apart and fly around the perimeter rather than go directly over a crop circle formation.

Researchers have spent a great deal of time investigating different aspects of crop circles. They try to detect traces of human involvement in the circle-making, test the area of the circle itself for geophysical anomalies, and analyze the field's grain both from within and outside the circles, searching for differences.

Dr. W. C. Levengood of BLT Research in Cambridge, Massachusetts, has analyzed many grain samples and confirmed, time after time, significant changes at the cellular level of crop circle plants. The plants from the circles have elongated cells and blown-out growth nodes. Seeds from the circle plants often show accelerated growth rates when they are sown, and in some instances, quite different-looking plants result. In many instances it appears that a vortex-like energy causes the plants to swirl down, flattening the design into the land. Whatever this energy is, it does not generally inhibit the plants' growth. They continue to show normal response to the sun, raising upward over several days following the appearance of the circle. Michael Chorost of Duke University found occasions of short-lived radionuclides in the top layer of soil in some of the formations. A British government laboratory found diminished nitrogen and decreased nematode populations as well as decreased water content in the soil of a formation. Researchers have discovered other anomalies as well, such as curious embedded magnetic particles and charred tissue. Some of the plant stalks within the circles show evidence of being exposed to rapid microwave heating.

Scientists have attempted to explain crop circles as a result of natural processes. One popular theory, accepted by many mainstream scientists and academics, is known as 'Plasma Vortex Theory'. Developed by Dr. Terence Mearden, it theorizes that electrified air (plasma), on the side of hills, becomes mini-tornadoes and screws down onto the ground, creating the circles. The theory also holds that the electrified air would cause a light to appear above the circle and therefore account for UFO sightings. Although this theory still has considerable support it has come under fire because of the highly intricate and complex crop circle patterns that have appeared since 1991. Another theory is that the circles are all hoaxes or practical jokes. Major support came to this theory when, on September 9, 1991, two Englishmen claimed to have created approximately 250 crop circles. However, those circles were more ragged than others, and many were already suspect. It is irrational to believe that all crop circles are faked for publicity or other reasons. Many crop circles appeared long before the phenomenon gained large recognition from the public and press. Too many circles and patterns are formed each year in too many countries for them to have been hoaxes. Many crop circles show strange mathematical traits when analyzed.

The crop circle phenomenon is an enigma. Many dollars have been spent by researchers and their associations in an attempt to find a solution to this intriguing puzzle which will continue to haunt humanity until an explanation is found.

Questions 15–27

Questions 15–19
Do the following statements reflect the claims of the writer of this passage?

Write:

YES	*if the statement reflects the claims of the writer.*
NO	*if the statement contradicts the writer.*
NOT GIVEN	*if it is impossible to say what the writer thinks about this.*

[15] Crop circles only appear in wheat fields.

[16] Crop circles have never been documented in tropical countries.

[17] The largest number of crop circle reportings in a single year occurred in 1990.

[18] The patterns of crop circles have become increasingly complex over the years.

[19] All crop circles are hoaxes.

Questions 20–23
*Complete the summary below. Choose **NO MORE THAN THREE WORDS FROM THE PASSAGE** for each answer.*

Since the early 1970's, over ten thousand crop circles have been reported around the world, the greatest number in **[20]** .... , where in a single year, over one hundred circles appeared. Phenomena such as the appearance of strange lights and unusual **[22]** .... sometimes occur around the sites of crop circles. **[22]** .... are not affected but it has been observed that birds **[23]** .... flying over a formation.

Questions 24–27

*Use the information in the text to match one scientist (**A–C**) with each area of study (24–27) listed below.*

A   Dr. Mearden
B   Dr. Levengood
C   Michael Chorost

EXAMPLE	
	Answer
observations of light in relation to crop circles	A

[24] changes in the structure of soil within crop circles

[25] accelerated growth of seeds from crop circles

[26] electrical charges in the air around crop circles

[27] changes in cell structure of plants found in crop circles

Passage 3

You should spend about 20 minutes on Questions 28–40 which are based on this passage.

ARE THESE TWO REPORTERS ON THE SAME PLANET?

An essay by scientist, educator and environmentalist, Dr. David Suzuki

A number of books, articles and television programs have disputed the reality of the claimed hazards of global warming, overpopulation, deforestation and ozone depletion. Two newspaper commentaries show the profound differences of opinion on critical issues affecting the planet.

The first, by Robert Kaplan, has generated both fear and denial. Entitled *The Coming Anarchy*, the report paints a horrifying picture of the future for humanity. The author suggests that the terrible consequences of the conjunction between exploding human population and surrounding environmental degradation are already visible in Africa and parts of Southeast Asia. As society is destabilised by the AIDS epidemic, government control evaporates, national borders crumble beneath the pressure of environmental refugees and local populations revert to tribalism to settle old scores or defend against fleeing masses and bands of stateless nomads on the move.

Kaplan believes what he has seen in Africa and Southeast Asia is the beginning of a global pattern of disintegration of social, political and economic infrastructure under the impact of ecological degradation, population pressure and disease. As ecosystems collapse, this scenario could sweep the planet, first in Eastern Europe and then the industrialised countries. It is a frightening scenario, built on a serious attempt to project the aftermath of ecological destruction. It comes from a core recognition that the planet is finite and consumption has vast social, political and economic ramifications. It has also generated a great deal of discussion and controversy.

Marcus Gee pronounces Kaplan's vision 'dead wrong' in a major article headlined *Apocalypse Deferred*. Attacking the 'doomsayers', Gee counters with the statistics favoured by believers in the limitless benefits and potential of economic growth. Citing the spectacular improvements in human health, levels of education and literacy, availability of food and length of life even in the developing world, Gee pronounces the fivefold increase in the world economy since 1950 as the cause of this good news. He does concede that immense problems remain, from ethnic nationalism to tropical deforestation to malnutrition to cropland losses but concludes that Kaplan has exaggerated many of the crises and thus missed the broad pattern of progress.

Focusing on statistics of the decline in child mortality and the rise in longevity, food production and adult literacy, Gee reaches the conclusion that things have never been better. Economic indicators, such as the rise in gross world product and total exports show 'remarkable sustained and dramatic progress'. Life for the majority of the world's citizens is getting steadily better in almost every category.'

Gee's conclusions rest heavily on economic indicators. He points out the annual 3.9 percent rise in the global economy and the more than doubling of the gross output per person, that has occurred for the past thirty years. World trade has done even better, growing by 6 percent annually between 1960 and 1990 as tariffs have declined from 40 percent of a product's price in 1947 to 5% today.

Gee skips lightly over such facts as third world debt and the daily toll of 22,000 child deaths from easily preventable disease. He also fails to mention that during this period the gulf between rich and poor countries has increased. He does acknowledge the threats of loss of topsoil and forests, pollution of the air, and contamination of water. However, he concludes that there is little evidence they are serious enough to halt or even reverse human progress. Gee challenges the notion of a population crisis since there have never been as many people so well off. Furthermore, he suggests there will never be a limit to population because more people means more Einsteins to keep making life better.

Gee's outlook rests on a tiny minority of scientists who have faith in the boundless potential of science and technology to overcome the physical constraints of air, water and soil so that a much larger population can be sustained. His final proof? – the general rise in living standard along with population growth. But the relationship between changes in living standard and population is a correlation, not proof of causal connection. Gee is ignoring basic economic as well as scientific reality.

If we inherit a bank account with a thousand dollars that earns 5% interest annually, we could withdraw fifty dollars or less each year forever. However suppose we start to increase our withdrawals, say up to sixty dollars, then seventy dollars and more each year. For many years the account would yield cash. But it would be foolish to conclude that we could keep drawing more from the account indefinitely. Yet that is what Gee believes. As ocean fisheries around the world show, we are using up the ecological capital of the planet (biodiversity, air, water, soil) rather than living off the interest. It is a dangerous deception to believe that the human-created artifice called economics can keep the indicators rising as the life support systems of the planet continue to decline.

The value system that dominates most of the popular media promotes the delusion that resources and the economy can continue to expand indefinitely. It also blinds the public to the urgency and credibility of warnings that an environmental crisis confronts us.

Questions 28–40

Questions 28–33

Use the information in the passage to match the people (**A–C**) with the opinions (**28–33**) listed below. There may be more than one correct answer.

    A   R. Kaplan, author of *The Coming Anarchy*
    B   M. Gee, author of *Apocalypse Deferred*
    C   D. Suzuki, author of this passage

EXAMPLE	*Answer*
Environmental challenges will be met by technological advances.	*B*

[28] Our patterns of consumption are using up the ecological capital of the planet.

[29] Crises beginning in the Third World will spread to developed countries.

[30] Scientific progress will enable the planet to sustain increased population.

[31] Social and political infrastructure worldwide could collapse.

[32] Earth's life support systems are at critical risk.

[33] Environmental problems are not a threat to progress.

Questions 34–36

Choose **ONE** phrase from the list below (**A–G**) to complete each of the following sentences. There are more phrases than questions so you will not use all of them.

[34] The growth of world trade...

[35] The relationship between population and standard of living ...

[36] Natural resources and the economy...

List of Phrases

A   have most benefited developing countries

B   has led to a drop in the standard of living generally

C   cannot continue to expand indefinitely

D   have decreased third world debt

E   shows a correlation, not cause and effect

F   pose a threat to human progress

G   has been accompanied by a fall in tariffs

Questions 37–40

*Choose the correct letter **A–D**.*

[37] Which of the following is **NOT** stated by Kaplan as a key contributing factor to potential global destabilisation?

    A   political corruption

    B   collapse of ecosystems

    C   population explosion

    D   malnutrition and disease

[38] What is the main source of Gee's optimism?

    A   scientific and technological advances

    B   decreasing Third World debt

    C   the rise in the standard of living worldwide

    D   economic growth

[39] Which of the following can we infer about the views of the author of this passage?

    A   He disagrees with both Gee and Kaplan.

    B   He supports the views of Gee.

    C   His views are closer to those of Kaplan.

    D   He thinks both Gee and Kaplan are right.

[40] The main purpose of the author in this passage is...

    A   to alert us to an environmental crisis.

    B   to educate the media.

    C   to create uncertainty about the future.

    D   to challenge current economic theory.

Passage 1

You should spend about 20 minutes on Questions 1–13 which are based on this passage.

Lake Vostok

A Beneath the white blanket of Antarctica lies half a continent of virtually uncharted territory – an area so completely hidden that scientists have little clue what riches await discovery. Recently, Russian and British glaciologists identified an immense lake – one of Earth's largest and deepest – buried beneath 4,000 meters of ice immediately below Russia's Vostok Station.

B As details have emerged, a growing number of scientists are showing interest, with dozens of investigators keen to explore the feature, known as Lake Vostok. A thick layer of sediment at the bottom of the lake could hold novel clues to the planet's climate going back tens of millions of years. By looking at the ratio of different oxygen isotopes, scientists should be able to trace how Earth's temperature changed over the millennia. NASA has expressed interest in Lake Vostok because of its similarity to Europa. This moon of Jupiter appears to have a water ocean covered by a thick ice sheet, measuring perhaps tens of kilometers in depth. If hydrothermal vents exist beneath the ice, chemical reactions on Europa could have created the molecular building blocks for life, if not life itself. Vostok would be an ideal testing ground for technology that would eventually fly to Europa or places even more distant, say many scientists. Though cheap compared with a Europan mission, any expedition to Vostok would represent a significant investment.

C Vostok Station holds the uncomfortable distinction of having recorded the coldest temperature on Earth. Thermometers there measured –89.6°C in July 1983, and the average temperature hovers around –55°C. It's the thick ice, strangely, that enables a lake to survive in such a frozen environment. The 4 kilometers of ice acts effectively as an insulating blanket protecting the bedrock underneath the ice from the cold temperatures above. Geothermal heat coming from the planet's interior keeps the lake from freezing and warms the lowest layers of ice. The tremendous weight of the ice sheet also plays a role in maintaining the lake. Beneath 4 km of glacier, the pressure is intense enough to melt ice at a temperature of –4°C. These factors have helped lakes develop across much of the thickly blanketed East Antarctica. To date more than 70 hidden lakes have been detected in the small portion of the continent. Lake Vostok is the largest of these, stretching 280 km from south to north and some 60 km from east to west. At Vostok station, which sits at the southern end of the lake, the water depth appears to be 500 m according to seismic experiments carried out by Russian researchers.

D The first clues to Lake Vostok's existence came in the 1970s, when British, U.S., and Danish researchers collected radar observations by flying over this region. The radar penetrates the ice and bounces off whatever sits below. When researchers found a surface as flat as a mirror, they surmised that a lake must exist underneath the ice. An airborne survey of the lake is being undertaken, the first step toward eventually drilling into the water. Along with the potential rewards come a host of challenges. Researchers must find a way to penetrate the icy covering without introducing any microorganisms or pollutants into the sealed-off water.

E What about life in the depths? If tiny microbes do populate the lake, they may be some of the hungriest organisms ever discovered. Lake Vostok has the potential to be one of the most energy-limited, or oligotropic, environments on the planet. For the lake's residents, the only nutrients would come from below. Russian investigators have speculated that the lake floor may have hot springs spewing out hydrothermal fluids stocked with reduced metals and other sorts of chemical nutrients. Scant geological evidence available for this region, however, indicates that the crust is old and dead. Without a stream of nutrients seeping up from the deep Earth, the only potential source of energy lies above the lake. The ice sheet above the water is creeping from west to east at a rate of roughly four metres per year. The lowermost layers of ice melt when they come in contact with the lake, liberating trapped gases and bits of crushed-up rock. If the glacier recently passed over rock before reaching the lake, it could be supplying organic compounds useful to microorganisms. It also could be seeding the lake with a continuous source of new residents. Bacteria, yeasts, fungi, algae, and even pollen grains have been found in the Vostok ice core samples taken down to depths of 2,750 m – three quarters of the way to the bottom. At least some of these organisms are alive and capable of growing, according to recent reports. The results of this analysis may indirectly indicate whether anything survives in the lightless body of water.

Questions 1–13

Questions 1–4

The passage has 5 sections A–E. Choose the most suitable heading for sections B–E from the list of headings below. Write the appropriate numbers (i–viii). There are more headings than sections so you will not use all of them.

List of Headings

(i)	Cost of exploration
(ii)	Location and description of the lake
(iii)	Potential for living organisms in the lake
(iv)	Challenges of exploration
(v)	Discovery of the lake
(vi)	Possible sources of nutrients to support life
(vii)	Types of organisms in the lake
(viii)	Scientific interest in Lake Vostok

EXAMPLE	
	Answer
Section **A**	**v**

[1] Section **B**

[2] Section **C**

[3] Section **D**

[4] Section **E**

Questions 5–6
*Choose the correct letter **A–D**.*

[5] Which is **NOT** given as a reason for interest in exploring Lake Vostok?

  A   to test technology for space exploration
  B   to develop anti-pollution devices
  C   to investigate the history of Earth's climate
  D   to look for living organisms

[6] Lake Vostok does not freeze because...

  A   a thick ice cover provides insulation.
  B   it is warmed by heat from the earth's surface.
  C   low pressure prevents freezing.
  D   an underwater volcano erupted recently.

Questions 7–13
Do the following statements reflect the claims of the author?

Write:

YES	*if the statement reflects the author's claims.*
NO	*if the statement contradicts the author's claims.*
NOT GIVEN	*if the information is not clearly given in the passage.*

[7]   Only one lake has been found beneath Antarctica.

[8]   Lake Vostok was detected by radar.

[9]   Exploration of Lake Vostok is coordinated by Russia.

[10] Nutrients to support life have been found in the Antarctic ice.

[11] The ice above the lake is moving to the east.

[12] Scientists have drilled through the ice into the water of Lake Vostok.

[13] The water in the lake is approximately 500 m deep at the southern end.

Passage 2

You should spend about 20 minutes on Questions 14–27 which are based on this passage.

The cells from hell

Recently, an international team of biologists met to discuss what they believe is a global crisis in the sudden appearance of strange marine micro-organisms capable of poisoning not just fish but people too.

In the mid-1980s, fishermen in North Carolina, on the eastern coast of the United States, began complaining about mysterious fish kills. They were convinced that pollution was responsible but nobody would listen. That changed in 1988 after an accident at a research center. Tank after tank of fish suddenly died. Researchers spotted an unknown micro-organism in the water. It was later named *pfiesteria.*

Pfiesteria belongs to a prehistoric group of algae, that are part plant, part animal. They are called *dinoflagellates* after the tiny whips or flagella that propel them through the water. Magnified a thousand times they are some of the strangest and most beautiful creatures in the sea. They are at the bottom of the food chain but, to deter fish from swallowing them, some have evolved powerful toxins.

As the researchers were to discover, pfiesteria doesn't just discourage fish. It actively hunts them, then eats them. Fish are one of its preferred foods but one of the intriguing things about pfiesteria is that it will eat everything from bacteria to dead plant and animal remains all the way up to mammalian tissues. So its food spans the entire food web of an estuary. Gradually the researchers realised that nothing in the water was safe from pfiesteria. It could harm humans too. A mis-directed air-conditioning duct from a room containing the toxins nearly killed one of the researchers. He suffered a host of symptoms ranging from profuse sweating, tingling hands and feet, to liver and kidney problems, as well as memory loss.

As the research intensified, some startling discoveries were made. In tanks, pfiesteria was quite content to behave like a plant and photosynthesize. However when fish were added a dramatic transformation occurred. Pfiesteria switched to attack mode. In a matter of minutes it changed shape and secreted a toxin. The fish quickly became disorientated and within five minutes all were dead. Pfiesteria changed shape again and devoured them. When it had had its fill it vanished. No one had ever seen an organism do this.

Initially scientists believed this was part of a natural cycle, but on closer examination, it seemed pollution was to blame. When the water containing the biggest fish kills was analysed, scientists found high levels of pollution. But this is just one of the factors that can boost the transformation in pfiesteria. Others include large numbers of fish travelling together which feed in poorly flushed places with a lot of algae to eat and other rich food sources. That is the perfect habitat for pfiesteria.

But pfiesteria is not the only concern. In the oceans all around the world similar kinds of algae are now materialising and turning toxic. In the last decade these algal blooms[1] have poisoned sea-lions in California, caused catastrophic fish kills in the Pacific, the Mediterranean and the North Sea, and devastated the shellfish industry in New Zealand. Researchers from forty seven nations met recently to share the latest information about harmful algal blooms. They heard about new kinds of toxins and discussed possible links between algae and whale strandings. But what dominated the proceedings was news that toxic algae are spreading to new shores in ballast water carried by ships.

That may have already happened in Australian waters. A tuna kill in 1996 cost fish farmers an estimated $45 million. The official explanation was that a storm was to blame. But there were also reports of orange-brown streaks in the water. When a water sample was examined, it was found to be teeming with an alga never before seen in Australia, called *chattonella*. The same chattonella killed half a billion dollars' worth of fish in Japan in 1972. This toxin was also present in the livers of the dead tuna. Despite this powerful evidence, the official explanation remains that a storm was the killer. However, in Japan this was a prime example of an algal bloom induced by the waste products of the aquaculture industry itself, and of course that is not something that the tuna industry wants to hear.

It is clear that chattonella is present in Australian waters. But there is little knowledge of what else may surface or where it may have come from. What is of greater concern is that, in Australia and around the world, there is a reluctance to acknowledge that it is human activity which is triggering the transformation of normally benign organisms into increasingly dangerous forms. If we continue to mismanage the way nutrients and pollutants are released into the environment we will have to confront new versions of the cells from hell.

Glossary

[1] algal bloom   The rapid growth under specific conditions, of minute aquatic plants.

Questions 14 –26

Questions 14–17

Complete the summary below. Choose your answers from the box below the summary. There are more words than you need so you will not use all of them.

> **EXAMPLE**
>
> Pfiesteria is a ......*micro-organism*...... with some unusual characteristics. Under normal

conditions, it acts like a **[14]** .... but it has also developed powerful

[15] .... as a defence against being eaten by fish. When the fish are

disabled and killed by the neurotoxins, the organism **[16]** .... them.

Then it **[17]** ....

List of words

jaws	grows	animal
kills	eats	poisons
plant	disappears	micro-organism
bacteria	fish	dies

Questions 18–21

*Fill in the blanks with **NO MORE THAN THREE WORDS FROM THE PASSAGE.***

Conditions which favour the growth of toxic algae include high levels of

[18] .... and **[19]** .... fish feeding together. Research

scientists at the international conference learned about **[20]** .... toxic

algae and how they are spreading around the world in water **[21]** ....

Questions 22–26

Classify the following as:

A   *caused by pfiesteria*
B   *caused by chattonella*
C   *caused by an unidentified micro-organism*

EXAMPLE	*Answer*
Serious illness of researcher	*A*

[22] death of sea-lions off the coast of California (1990s)

[23] fish kill in Japan (1972)

[24] shellfish industry losses in New Zealand (1990s)

[25] tuna industry losses in Australia (1990s)

[26] fish kill in North Carolina (1980s)

Passage 3

You should spend about 20 minutes on Questions 27–40 which are based on this passage.

Mystery of the mummies

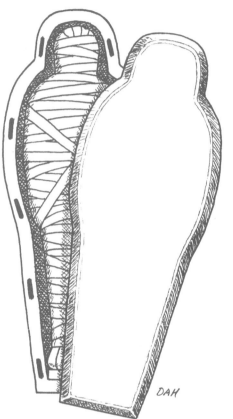

In 1992, a German scientist made a discovery which was to upset whole areas of scientific study from history and archeology to chemistry and botany. Dr. Svetlana Balabanova, a forensic specialist, was performing tissue tests on an Egyptian mummy, part of a German museum collection. The mummified remains were of a woman named *Henut-Taui* who had died over 3000 years ago. Amazingly, the tests revealed that her body contained large quantities of cocaine and nicotine. Dr. Balabanova had regularly used the same testing methods to convict people of drug consumption but she had not expected to find nicotine and coca in an Ancient Egyptian mummy. It is generally accepted that these two plants, native to the Americas did not exist on other continents prior to European exploration.

Dr. Balabanova repeated the tests then sent out fresh samples to three other labs. When the results came back positive she published a paper with two other scientists. If Balabanova was shocked by the results of her tests she was even more shocked at the hostile response to her publication. She received many insulting letters, accusing her of fraud.

There were two explanations that came immediately to mind. One was that something in the tests could have given a false result. The second was that the mummies tested were not truly Ancient Egyptian. Perhaps they were relatively modern bodies, containing traces of cocaine. Dr. Balabanova then examined tissue from 134 naturally preserved bodies over a thousand years old discovered in an excavated cemetery in the Sudan. About a third of them tested positive for nicotine or cocaine.

But something had happened even earlier which should have initiated serious discussion. In 1976 the mummified remains of Ramses II arrived in Paris for repair work. Dr. Michelle Lescot of the Natural History Museum (Paris) was looking at sections of bandages and within the fibres found a plant fragment. When she checked it under a microscope she was amazed to discover that the plant was tobacco. Fearing that she had made some mistake she repeated her tests again and again with the same result every time: a New World plant had been found on an Old World mummy. The results caused a sensation in Europe. Was it possible that a piece of tobacco had been dropped by chance from the pipe of some forgotten archaeologist? Dr. Lescot responded to this charge of contamination by carefully extracting new samples from the abdomen, with the entire process recorded on film. These samples, which could not be 'droppings', were then tested. Once again they were shown to be tobacco. The discovery of tobacco fragments in the mummified body of Ramses II should have had a profound influence upon our whole understanding of the relationship between Ancient Egypt and America but this piece of evidence was simply ignored. It raised too many questions and was too far outside of commonly accepted scientific views.

So now the question had returned. Could Ancient Egyptian trade have stretched all the way across the Atlantic Ocean? This was an idea so unbelievable it could only be considered after all the other possibilities had been eliminated. Could Egyptians have obtained imports from a place thousands of miles away, from a continent supposedly not discovered until thousands of years later? Was it possible that coca – a plant from South America had found its way to Egypt 3,000 years ago? If the cocaine found in mummies could not be explained by contamination, or fake mummies or by Egyptian plants containing it, there appeared to be another interesting possibility: a trade route with links all the way to the Americas.

The Egyptians did make great efforts to obtain incense and other valuable plants used in religious ceremonies and herbal medicines, but to the majority of archeologists, the idea is hardly worth talking about. Professor John Baines, an Egyptologist from Oxford University states: 'I don't think it is at all likely that there was an ancient trade network that included America. The essential problem with any such idea is that there are no artefacts ...found either in Europe or in America.' But other experts aren't so sure. Professor Martin Bernal, an historian, from Cornell University says, 'We're getting more and more evidence of world trade at an earlier stage. You have the Chinese silk definitely arriving in Egypt by 1000 BC.' In his opinion, it is arrogance on the part of modern people to believe that a transoceanic trading network could only have been set up in recent times.

The discoveries in the mummies from Egypt and Sudan have challenged conventional beliefs. It is no longer possible to exclude the hypothesis of transoceanic trade in ancient times. The tale of Henut Taui and the story of Ramses II show that, in science, facts can be rejected if they don't fit with our beliefs, while what is believed to be proven, may actually be uncertain. It is understandable then, how a story of a scientist, a few mummies and some routine tests, could upset whole areas of knowledge we thought we could take for granted.

Questions 27–40

Questions 27–29
*Choose the correct letter **A–D**.*

[27] What most surprised Dr. Balabanova about her discovery?

    A   the presence of drugs in the mummies
    B   the fact that the plants originated in the western hemisphere
    C   the positive results of tests on other mummies
    D   the hostile reaction of the scientific community

[28] Which of the following was ruled out by Dr. Lescot's investigation?

    A   Tobacco had been dropped onto the mummy.
    B   Tobacco grew in Ancient Egypt.
    C   Chemicals produced false test results.
    D   The mummies were fake.

[29] Why was the discovery of tobacco in the body of Ramses II ignored?

    A   Contamination was suspected.
    B   The evidence raised difficult questions.
    C   The tests produced false results.
    D   The researcher was a woman.

Questions 30–34

*Match **ONE** of the researchers **(A–D)** to each of the statements **(30–34)** below. There may be more than one correct answer.*

     A   Dr. Svetlana Balabanova

     B   Dr. Michelle Lescot

     C   Professor John Baines

     D   Professor Martin Bernal

[30]   first to find a substance from the Americas in a mummy

[31]   argues against transoceanic trade because of lack of evidence

[32]   had to defend against attacks on research methodology

[33]   gives evidence of extensive Egyptian trade in ancient times

[34]   publication of research results was controversial

Questions 35–39

Do the following statements reflect the opinions of the writer in the passage?

Write:

YES	*if the statement reflects the opinion of the writer.*
NO	*if the statement contradicts the writer.*
NOT GIVEN	*if it is impossible to say what the writer thinks about this.*

[35] There is proof that tobacco was grown in Ancient Egypt.

[36] Trade routes across the Atlantic Ocean may have existed thousands of years ago.

[37] Ancient Egyptians were great ship builders.

[38] The scientific community generally rejects the idea of contact between Ancient Egypt and the Americas.

[39] The unusual test results could have come from 'qat', a plant native to North Africa.

Question 40

*Choose the correct letter **A–D**.*

[40] What is the main idea of this passage?

    A   Experimental research often gives false results.
    B   Long-held beliefs can be challenged by new information.
    C   The scientific community is conservative by nature.
    D   Ideas which don't fit our belief system must be wrong.

FAST TRACK READING

LEARN FROM YOUR MISTAKES

Look again at your answers

You lose marks for small errors.
Mistakes like these can cost you easy marks.
Look at this example of an answer sheet.

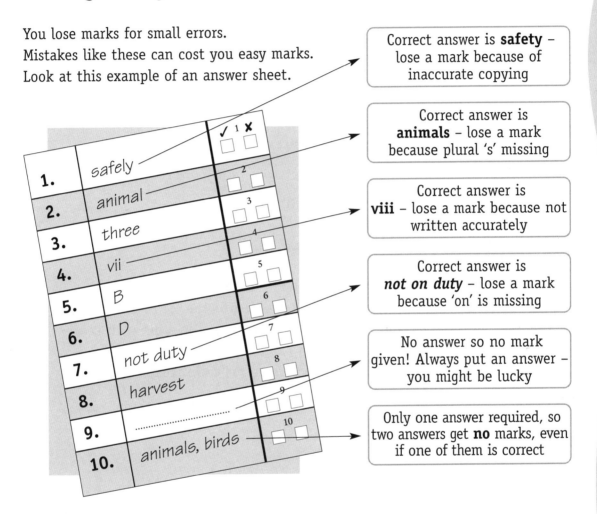

Correct answer is **safety** – lose a mark because of inaccurate copying

Correct answer is **animals** – lose a mark because plural 's' missing

Correct answer is **viii** – lose a mark because not written accurately

Correct answer is ***not on duty*** – lose a mark because 'on' is missing

No answer so no mark given! Always put an answer – you might be lucky

Only one answer required, so two answers get **no** marks, even if one of them is correct

Did you lose many marks in Practice Test 1 because of this kind of mistake? Don't throw away marks because you are in a hurry! A couple of errors like these could make all the difference to your final score!

Go back to the questions you got wrong

Try to analyse each mistake. Why did you write the wrong answer?

Did you?

- have problems understanding the words in the question?
- have problems understanding a word or phrase in the passage?
- choose an incorrect answer which was included to 'tempt' you?

If you still don't understand why an answer is incorrect, ask a teacher, a native speaker or another student to explain the answer to you.

Be sure you understand before starting the next test.

Try this... to build your vocabulary

Write down all new words and expressions.

- Keep a special notebook for new words and phrases.
- Check the meaning in your dictionary and with a teacher or native speaker.
- Find out any other meanings when the word(s) is used in a different context.
- Write a few examples using the word or expression.
- Ask a teacher or native speaker to check what you've written.

Make sure that you will understand the meaning if you read it in another test.

Collect synonyms.

- Note down words or phrases from the reading, with the same meaning as *different words* used in the question.

  eg: on Saturday and Sunday = at the weekend
  It was a cold, wet and windy day = the weather was pretty miserable.

Watch out for 'tricky' synonyms! If you got caught once, don't get caught again.

Practice reading to conquer time!

Another common reason for errors and/or a low score in the IELTS Reading Test is lack of time. Mistakes are made due to hurrying, and often candidates don't finish the test in the time allowed.

So to improve your test results you need to work both quickly and accurately ...and conquer time!

Pace yourself

- Practise spending no more than 20 minutes per section, aim for less.
- Don't waste marks (remember?) so be sure you get all the *easier* answers correct.
- Don't spend too long on one question, mark it and come back later.
- Don't leave any question unanswered. Guess. You might be lucky!

Read what you need

Learn to **skim and scan:**
- Skim for the part of the passage that seems related to the question by looking at headings, sub-headings and topic sentences (usually the first sentence of a paragraph).
- Scan by looking carefully at that part to find the specific information.

Practice makes perfect ...

- to get to know question and answer types.
- to increase your vocabulary.
- to spot the synonyms.
- to pace yourself through the test.

HOW CAN I IMPROVE?

You need to read efficiently for success in IELTS.

What to read first...
- First look quickly at the reading text: its title, sub headings, tables, diagrams. What's it about?
- Then look quickly at the first few questions. How many are there? What kind?
- There's no time to memorise them, but your brain will be more focussed.
- Now read the text quickly and then go back to the questions.

Adapt the way you read to the type of question.

- **'Whole text' questions** such as choosing headings for paragraphs or sections

  First read the topic sentences. These should tell you what the paragraphs are about. If the topic sentence and the heading seem similar, then read the paragraph slowly. and carefully to check that they go together.

- **'Detail' questions** such as multiple choice questions (choose A, B, C or D)

  First skim to find which part of the text seems to be about that information. When you locate that part of the text, scan carefully for the specific detail you need. NB There will always be an answer that is wrong, but put in to try and tempt you, (the 'red herring' answer) so double check that you've chosen the right one!

Practise skimming for names and numbers

- If the question asks for the name of a place, city, country, street, person or organisation, they're quite easy to find because they always start with a capital letter.

- Remember the different ways to write numbers: nine or 9 or (ix) or IX, 1,400 or one thousand four hundred or fourteen hundred or 1400 (the year).

- Be sure you're familiar with how decimals and fractions are written in English.

If you don't understand a word or phrase...

Don't panic!
Try to guess from the nouns and verbs around it.
Look for words like 'similarly' or 'in contrast to' or 'unlike' which may help you.

By taking the time to repeat the tests, you are developing your reading skills, building vocabulary and increasing your understanding of test strategies. This is time well spent.

TIPS FROM TEST-TAKERS

Never Stop

'I never stop practising my reading in English. When I'm on the bus, train or walking, I always try to understand the signs, posters and advertisements. If I don't understand, I write it in a notebook so that I can ask a friend or my teacher.'

Tip from Yi Ling

'I was very slow at reading and thought I could never finish the test in one hour. But I made myself do a practice test every weekend. After a couple of months I began to recognise the kind of questions and how to find the answers more quickly. I was always careful with the easier questions at the beginning of the test. When I did the IELTS exam I got a 6!'

Fall In Love

'I'm 'in love' with my dictionary! I bought a really good dictionary. It was quite expensive, but I use it every day so I don't feel guilty about how much it cost. I try to check everything I don't understand.'

Tip from Andrea who scored 7 on the IELTS Reading Test

'The first time I took the test there were many words I didn't understand so I only scored a 5. I bought a small address book with pages marked A-Z, and every day I wrote down new words or expressions I didn't know. I tested myself every night. If I could remember what the word meant three days running I crossed it out. After three months, when I took the test again, I had a much bigger vocabulary and I got a much better score!'

Answer all the questions

'I put an answer, even if I really didn't understand. If it's a multiple choice then there are only 4 possible answers, so I chose an answer that seemed to make sense and was grammatically correct.'

Keep cool

'Remember that every question scores one mark, but the questions generally increase in difficulty as you go from 1 to 40. So I didn't worry too much about the last few questions, but I was careful with the earlier ones.'

IELTS LISTENING AND READING ANSWER SHEET

Module taken:

Academic ☐ General Training ☐

Version number:

Please enter the number in the boxes and shade the number in the grid

00 10 20 30 40 50 60 70 80 90
☐ ☐ ☐ ☐ ☐ ☐ ☐ ☐ ☐ ☐

0 1 2 3 4 5 6 7 8 9
☐ ☐ ☐ ☐ ☐ ☐ ☐ ☐ ☐ ☐

		✓ 1 ✗
1.		☐ ☐
2.		☐ 2 ☐
3.		☐ 3 ☐
4.		☐ 4 ☐
5.		☐ 5 ☐
6.		☐ 6 ☐
7.		☐ 7 ☐
8.		☐ 8 ☐
9.		☐ 9 ☐
10.		☐ 10 ☐
11.		☐ 11 ☐
12.		☐ 12 ☐
13.		☐ 13 ☐
14.		☐ 14 ☐
15.		☐ 15 ☐
16.		☐ 16 ☐
17.		☐ 17 ☐
18.		☐ 18 ☐
19.		☐ 19 ☐
20.		☐ 20 ☐
21.		☐ 21 ☐

		✓ 22 ✗
22.		☐ ☐
23.		☐ 23 ☐
24.		☐ 24 ☐
25.		☐ 25 ☐
26.		☐ 26 ☐
27.		☐ 27 ☐
28.		☐ 28 ☐
29.		☐ 29 ☐
30.		☐ 30 ☐
31.		☐ 31 ☐
32.		☐ 32 ☐
33.		☐ 33 ☐
34.		☐ 34 ☐
35.		☐ 35 ☐
36.		☐ 36 ☐
37.		☐ 37 ☐
38.		☐ 38 ☐
39.		☐ 39 ☐
40.		☐ 40 ☐
41.		☐ 41 ☐
42.		☐ 42 ☐
Band Score		**Total**

UNIT 3 WRITING

WHAT'S AHEAD...
IN THE WRITING UNIT

- The IELTS Writing Test

- What is the examiner looking for?

- Examiners' Suggestions

- *Fast Track Writing*

  - More about Task 1

  - More about Task 2

- Instructions for Test Practice

- Writing Tests 1-6

  Activities and Sample Answer
  for each writing task

THE IELTS WRITING TEST

Each Writing Test consists of two tasks to be completed in 1 hour.

TASK 1

Write a report describing a diagram or table.

Time: 20 minutes
Length: 150 words minimum

What skills are needed?
• read and understand the diagram/table
• organise the information into connected sentences
• write clearly and accurately in an academic style

WHAT IS THE EXAMINER LOOKING FOR?

Assessment Criteria	In other words...
Task fulfilment	Have you done what the question asks, without leaving out important details?
Coherence/Cohesion	Do sentences connect information effectively? Is there good paragraph structure and organisation? Is the information easy to follow?
Sentence Structure/ Vocabulary	Is there a variety of sentence types? Is the grammar accurate? Is the vocabulary accurate and appropriate?

TASK 2

Write an essay to develop an argument, express a point of view or solve a problem.

Time: 40 minutes
Length: 250 words minimum

What skills are needed?
- read and understand the essay question
- generate ideas on the topic
- organise your ideas into paragraphs
- write clearly and accurately in an academic style

WHAT IS THE EXAMINER LOOKING FOR?

Assessment Criteria	In other words...
Argument/Ideas/ Evidence	Is the viewpoint relevant and clear? Are there enough ideas developed with examples to support them?
Communicative Quality	Is the answer fluent, easy to read and well-organised, in the style of an argument? Is the overall meaning clear?
Sentence Structure/ Vocabulary	Is there a variety of sentence types? Is the grammar accurate? Is the vocabulary appropriate?

EXAMINERS' SUGGESTIONS

Here's what IELTS examiners have to say about some of the most common problems they see in Writing Tests, along with suggestions for improvement.

Problems	Suggestions
Timing *Task 2 answers unfinished if too much time is spent on Task 1.*	Stop working on Task 1 after 20 minutes. Task 2 is worth more marks, so give yourself the full 40 minutes to complete your Task 2 answer.
Too short *If you write less than the minimum number of words for either task, you will lose marks.*	Practise regularly. Once you learn the essay patterns you will be able to write the required number of words without wasting time counting.
Off topic *An essay that doesn't address the topic will lose marks, even if it is well written.*	Keep going back to the task statement while planning and writing to make sure you relate your argument to the task as it is written.
Repetition *Saying the same thing in slightly different ways shows you don't have enough ideas.*	This is usually a problem of planning. Think of as many ideas as you can before you start to write. Decide on a topic for each paragraph and which examples to include.
Irrelevant information *Filling out an essay with information unrelated to the question won't get marks.*	Check back to the wording of the task. Is the idea/example relevant to the topic? Does it answer the question as given? If not, leave it out.
Mixed up *Some essays have too many ideas and too little organization. They are difficult to follow.*	Stick to one main idea per paragraph, stated clearly in the topic sentence. Use the rest of the paragraph to develop and support that idea with examples.
Unreadable *It is impossible to give a good mark, if the writing is illegible.*	Be kind to the examiner: • draw a line under your plan to separate it from the answer. • leave space between paragraphs. • cross out words neatly. • write legibly!

FAST TRACK WRITING

More about Task 1 ... and how to do it

Task 1 is about describing information given in the form of a pie chart/ table/ graph or process diagram /flow chart. The differences are outlined below. In the report you may add an opinion or comment in the conclusion but the main task is to summarise and describe. Often a Task 1 will combine two types of diagrams. Write about both and show the relationship between them.

Think First

	Pie charts/graphs, tables	Process diagrams/flow charts
Analyse the Task	Highlight key words. Note all headings, rates and measurements. Select the most important trends. Choose the best examples and summarise.	Highlight key words from task description. Note all labels and the order of steps. Describe the process step by step from beginning to end. Leave nothing out.
Ask questions	What is the purpose of this graph? What changes have occurred over time? What are the significant trends? What is the most interesting feature?	What is the purpose of this process? How does it work? How to include alternative steps? What is the end result?

Then Write

	Pie charts/graphs, tables	Process diagrams/flow charts
Introduction	Paraphrase the task description in 1 or 2 sentences. Don't copy it.	Paraphrase the task description in 1 or 2 sentences. Include the purpose/ end product of the process.
Description	Focus on trends and interesting points. Describe the most significant data first. Give examples to support trends. Use statistics accurately.	Follow each step in sequence. Include every step. Expand headings into sentences. Use connecting words to link steps.
Conclusion	Does not have to be a separate paragraph. A single sentence can round off your report. Include comment/ opinion/ interesting observation if appropriate.	Does not have to be a separate paragraph. A single sentence can round off your report. Include comment/ opinion/ interesting observation if appropriate.

To build your writing skills it is a good idea to work through all six of the Task 1s before starting the Task 2s.

More about Task 2 ... and how to do it

Task 2 essays require you to explore issues by comparing, evaluating or challenging ideas. You may be asked to present an argument or offer a solution to a problem. This means demonstrating your understanding of the topic by including examples and evidence. You should think of your audience as a non-specialist, educated reader. The main essay types are outlined below.

Step 1 Analyse the task

- Know the main **essay types** and what you have to do for each one.
- Read and highlight / underline **key words** related to (1) the topic and (2) the task.
- If necessary, explain key terms in your introduction.

Essay Types	Task words	This means...
Problem/solution	*What can be done to solve...?* *How can this problem be addressed?* *What challenges...?* *What strategies ...?*	Explain 2 or 3 aspects of the issue. (1 paragraph each) Suggest solutions. Make recommendations.
Agree or disagree	*Do you agree or disagree? Why?* *Explain your position.* *Justify your opinion.*	Take a position. Defend it strongly. Give several reasons to support your argument. (1 paragraph each) It is useful to acknowledge the opposite view (counter argument) and say why you don't accept it.
Two sides of an argument	*Discuss* *Compare/contrast* *Advantages/disadvantages*	Give a balanced presentation. This means you should write equally about both sides of the issue. In the conclusion you can indicate your position.
Make choices and justify	*From options A, B, C, D, E etc. choose 3 most important.* *Justify your choice.*	Each of your choices becomes the topic of one paragraph. Give reasons for choosing in this order.
Evaluate an argument	*To what extent...?* *How important...?* *What do you think?*	You will probably take a position which is neither in total agreement (100%) nor total disagreement (0%), but somewhere in between. Explain why.

Step 2 Generate ideas

Brainstorm:

Using Spider Diagrams

- Write key topic word(s) in the centre of a circle.
- Note down any related ideas or examples that come to mind.
- Do the same for other important words from the Task.
- Group the ideas to become your paragraph topics.

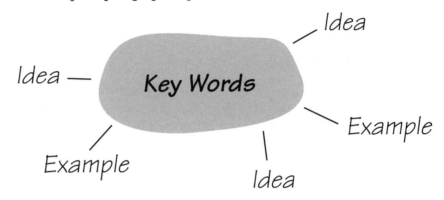

Or

Using Questions

- Start with key topic word(s).
- Think about the Task and ask relevant questions.
- Group the answers to become your paragraph topics.

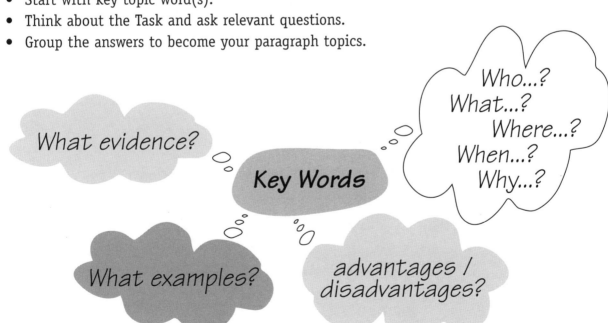

Step 3 Plan your Essay

Introduction	(1 short paragraph)	General statement(s) about the topic followed by **thesis statement** (what you are going to write about or what position you intend to take on the question.)
Body	(3–4 paragraphs)	Begin each paragraph with a **topic sentence** (main idea) followed by examples / evidence for support.
Conclusion	(1 short paragraph)	**Summarise,** but don't repeat, main ideas. Include recommendation if necessary or (re)-state your position, to bring essay to a close.

Beginning Task 2 practice?

- A good answer is more important than a fast one, so don't worry about time at first.
- It is more important to plan carefully and write a good answer.
- The more you practise, the faster and more proficient you will become.

Remember!

First plan **WHAT** you want to say:
   how many paragraphs
   what supporting evidence/ ideas to include
   what order to put them in

Then focus on **HOW** to say it.

As you write, think about:
   grammar
   vocabulary
   spelling
   punctuation

DON'T TRY TO DO BOTH AT ONCE

INSTRUCTIONS FOR TEST PRACTICE

There are SIX Writing Practice Tests

Test section format

Test papers are clearly marked in the next section.
Note: There are 3 pages of activities including a sample answer for Task 1 and Task 2 of each Writing Test.

To practise under test conditions

Total time allowed for each test (Task 1 plus Task 2): 60 minutes
DO NOT use a dictionary.

How to use this section

Test practice focus

Do a complete practice test (Task 1 and Task 2).
Compare your essays with the **Sample Answers.**
Use **Plan your answer** and **Build your language skills**
to improve organisation, grammar and vocabulary.
Re-write your essays if you have found ways to improve them.

Need more help?

Work through all Task 1s before beginning Task 2s.
Use **Plan your answer** to get started.
Do the activities in **Build your language skills.**
Study the **Sample Answer** and **Notes.**

...THEN write your own answer.

Sample Answers are a useful reference. However, try not to imitate them when you write your essays. Your own academic writing style will develop with practice.

You should spend about 20 minutes on this task.

> *The two pie charts below show changes in world population by region between 1900 and 2000.*
> *Write a report for a lecturer describing the information in these charts.*

Write at least 150 words.

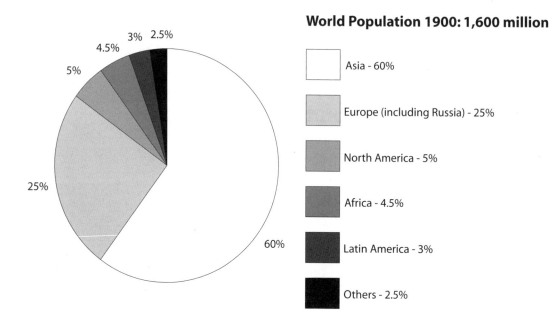

World Population 1900: 1,600 million

Asia - 60%

Europe (including Russia) - 25%

North America - 5%

Africa - 4.5%

Latin America - 3%

Others - 2.5%

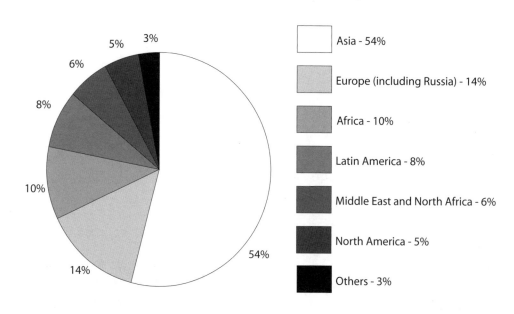

World Population 2000: 6 billion

Asia - 54%

Europe (including Russia) - 14%

Africa - 10%

Latin America - 8%

Middle East and North Africa - 6%

North America - 5%

Others - 3%

Analyse the task

Look at the question, title and subtitle.
Highlight key words.
Identify the main trends.

Think it through

Ask questions to find the information you need.
Then use the gapped sample answer as a guide.

Introduction

What kind of diagram is it?
What do the charts show?
Over what time period?
How are the regions shown?

These pie .... show changes in world population .... 1900 and 2000. The major regions .... represented as percentages of the total .... population.

Description

Where did the most significant change occur between 1900 and 2000?

From 1900 .... 2000 Africa's percentage of world population .... from 4.5% to 10% while Latin .... grew from 3% to 8% of world ....

Which 2 areas showed the greatest decreases and by how much?

On the .... hand, the percentage of population .... Europe and Asia decreased during the .... period. Europe dropped .... 25% to 14%, while Asia's percentage declined from 60% to 54%.

Which regions stayed the same?
What about the new category?

North .... however showed no change, remaining at .... of world population both in 1900 and 2000. The Middle East and North Africa, ... new category in 2000, represented .... of world population.

What about 'Others'?

The percentage of .... in the remaining areas of the .... ('Others') rose slightly from 2.5% to ....

Conclusion

What was the actual change in population?
Over what period?
What does this show?
How is it important/ interesting?

Overall, this represents a huge .... in the number of humans on the ...., from 1600 million to 6 billion .... just one hundred years. Most of this .... growth has occurred in developing ....

Complete these activities based on the sample answer to develop writing skills for Task 1 questions.

1   Synonyms

Find words or expressions in the sample answer that mean the same as:

- between 1900 and 2000 ....
- increase(d) ....
- decrease(d) ....
- show(ed) no change ....
- world population ....

2   Connecting words

Find 3 more words / expressions from the sample answer that are used to connect ideas, sentences and paragraphs.

1 eg *on the other hand* ....
2 ....
3 ....
4 ....

3   Prepositions

What prepositions follow each expression from the sample answer?

- ...world population increased .... 4.5% .... 10%.
- ...remaining .... 5%....
- ...this represents a huge increase .... the number of humans...
- Most .... this growth has occurred .... the developing world.

Answers: 1 from 1900 to 2000 / rose, grew / dropped, declined / remaining at / number of humans on the planet
2 while / however / overall **3** from, to / at / in / of, in

These pie charts show changes in world population between 1900 and 2000. The major regions are represented as percentages of the total world population.

From 1900 to 2000 Africa's percentage of world population increased from 4.5% to 10% while Latin America grew from 3% to 8% of world population. On the other hand, the percentage of population in Europe and Asia decreased during the same period. Europe dropped from 25% to 14% while Asia's percentage declined from 60% to 54%. North America, however, showed no change, remaining at 5% of world population both in 1900 and 2000. The Middle East and North Africa, a new category in 2000, represented 6% of world population. The percentage of population in the remaining areas of the world ('Others') rose slightly from 2.5% to 3%.

Overall, this represents a huge increase in the number of humans on the planet from 1,600 million to 6 billion in just one hundred years. Most of this population growth has occurred in developing countries.

(162 words)

Notes
- The pie chart and body of the report deal with percentages of population, not the actual number of people. Be sure you understand the difference.
- It would be incorrect to say 'Africa increased from 4.5% to 10 %' without adding 'of world population'. You could also say, 'Africa's percentage of world population increased from...'
- The actual change in the number of people in the world between 1900 and 2000 (1,600 million to 6 billion) is only mentioned in the conclusion.

You should spend about 40 minutes on this task.

Prepare a written argument for a well-educated reader on the following topic:

> *People today move to new cities or new countries more than ever before. What challenges do they experience? What strategies are there to meet these challenges?*

Write at least 250 words.

You should use your own ideas, knowledge and experience and support your arguments with examples and relevant evidence.

Step 1 Analyse the task

Read carefully to understand all the details.

What type of essay is it?

What are the key words...
    ...related to the topic?

    ...related to the task?

problem / solution

move / city / country

challenges / strategies

Step 2 Generate Ideas

Ask questions based on the key words.

What are the challenges?

Practical

Social

What strategies can help?

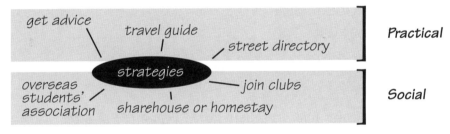

Practical

Social

Step 3 Think it through

Put your ideas in order before you start to write.

Introduction

Make a general statement about 'moving'.
Ask a question. 'Why do people move?'
Then answer it.

Paragraph topics

1 Practical challenges (travel, accommodation) and strategies

2 Social challenges (communication, stress) and strategies

Conclusion

summarise and re-state opinion

Complete these activities based on the sample answer to build writing skills for Task 2 questions.

1 Connecting words (who, which, that, where)

Find the sentences in the sample answer that combine each of the following pairs into one and write the connecting word used in each.

This is due to modern technology. Modern
technology makes travelling easier.

....

These provide challenges to someone. Someone
has not lived independently before.

....

It is helpful to get advice from someone. Someone
is familiar with the area.

....

There are travel guides. Travel guides give tips
and useful information.

....

There are other sports or hobby clubs. It is possible
to meet people in other sports or hobby clubs.

....

2 Before or After?

Do these little words in the sample answer refer to things stated before (B) or after (A) them?

These might present	**B / A**	many of these problems	**B / A**
such anxious moments	**B / A**	it is possible to...	**B / A**
it might be helpful	**B / A**		

3 Synonyms

Which word in each group is not a synonym of the others?

to move / to relocate / to change
useful / usable / handy
reasons / issues / challenges / problems
planning / preparing / starting

Answers: 1 which, who, who, which, where **2** B B B A B A **3** change / usable / reasons / starting

People today are clearly more mobile than in the past. This is largely due to modern technology which makes travelling and communicating easier and quicker. Why do people move? Often people re-locate to large cities for employment; some people study in English-speaking countries. Whatever the reason, moving away from home may create many challenges, both practical and social.

Firstly there are practical problems such as finding accommodation, managing finances, shopping and so on. These might present challenges to someone who has not lived independently before. In addition, adapting to a new city environment includes understanding the public transport system, possibly in another language, while trying not to get lost! The best strategy for minimising such anxious moments is to prepare in advance as much as possible. Thus it might be helpful to get advice from someone familiar with the area. There are also publications such as travel guides to overseas countries which give tips and useful information. A city street directory is also very handy. Ideally, sharing accommodation with someone who is familiar with the city, or staying in a 'homestay' on arrival in a new country, may overcome many of these problems. Homestay families or 'sharemates' will provide company and be able to explain aspects of the new city or culture that may seem strange at first.

There are also social and emotional issues to deal with, like loneliness or problems with the language. Moreover, starting a new job or course may be stressful at first. Generally, however, there are organisations such as overseas students' associations in an educational institution, or other sports or hobby clubs where it is possible to meet people and make friends.

In conclusion, although there are many challenges when leaving home for a new city or country, planning in advance can transform an ordeal into an adventure!

(304 words)

Notes

- Introduction starts with a general statement, then suggests some more specific details (why people are mobile). Finally a 'thesis statement' previews the body of the essay (the practical and social challenges). The writer avoids copying sentences from task prompt.
- First paragraph details **practical** challenges and strategies. Second paragraph deals with **social** challenges and strategies. An alternative essay plan could be one paragraph on challenges and one paragraph on strategies.

You should spend about 20 minutes on this task.

The table below shows personal savings as a percentage of personal income for selected countries in 1970, 1990 and 2000.
Write a report for a lecturer describing the information in the table.

Write at least 150 words.

Personal savings as a percentage of personal income

	1970	1990	2000
Canada	5.6	11.5	1.9
France	18.7	12.5	13.6
Germany	13.8	13.8	11.8*
Italy	29.5	17.6	11.4
Japan	17.6	12.1	13.6
UK	9.2	8.2	11.1
USA	8.2	5.5	4.0

*2000 percentage is for Germany post reunification

Analyse the task

Look at the question, title and subtitle.
Highlight key words.
Identify the main trends.

Think it through

Ask questions to find the information you need.
Then use the gapped sample answer as a guide.

Introduction

What does the table show?
...for how many countries?
...over what period?

> The table shows the .... of personal income devoted to .... in seven countries in 1970, 1990 and 2000.

Description

Which countries show the greatest change?

> The .... dramatic changes are .... in Italy, Japan, France and Canada.

For 1970, which country has the highest rate of saving?
(from highest to lowest)

> In 1970 Italy .... the highest savings rate of 29.5%, ... by France .... 18.7% and then Japan with 17.6%. Canada had the .... - 5.6%.

For 1990 ?
(from highest to lowest)

> By 1990 Italy was .... the leading country, though .... savings rate had dropped .... 17.6%. Germany was next .... 13.8% (same .... 1970) and the .... in France and Japan .... close behind. In Canada, ... savings rate had almost .... to 11.5%. The UK .... the USA had the .... rates, 8.2% and 5.5% ....

For 2000?
(from highest to lowest)

> .... 2000 the savings rates .... levelled out considerably across .... seven countries. France and .... led with 13.6%, followed .... Germany, Italy and the .... at around 11%. Personal .... in North America dropped .... , with the USA at .... and Canada at a .... low 1.9%.

Conclusion

What is the importance of these statistics?

> The overall .... shows a reduction .... savings over this 30 .... period.

Possible explanation for trend?
(include if additional words are needed)

> This probably indicates a .... in consumer confidence. People .... more willing to spend .... income or invest it, ... of leaving it in the bank.

Complete these activities based on the sample answer to build writing skills for Task 1 questions.

1   Sequencing statistics

Use these 5 expressions to complete a mini-text about five countries, A to E:

in last place,   followed by,   leading,   next,   close behind

Mini-text

A is the .... country, ... B. C is .... , with D .... is E.

2   Synonyms

Which expressions in the sample answer have the same meaning?

Expression	Sample answer expression
most significant	....
variations	....
can be seen	....
stabilised	....
fell dramatically	....

3   'most ....'   OR   ' –est'?

Write the superlative form of these adjectives from the sample answer.

Adjective	Superlative form
dramatic	....
low	....
high	....
evident	....
close	....

Answers: **1** A is the leading country, followed by B. C is next, with D close behind. In last place is E. **2** most significant – most dramatic / variations - changes / can be seen - are evident / stabilised – levelled out / fell dramatically – dropped sharply **3** most dramatic / lowest / highest / most evident / closest

The table shows the percentage of personal income devoted to savings in seven countries in 1970, 1990 and 2000.

The most dramatic changes are evident in Italy, Japan, France and Canada. In 1970 Italy had the highest savings rate of 29.5%, followed by France with 18.7% and Japan with 17.6%. Canada had the lowest rate – 5.6%.

By 1990 Italy was still the leading country, though its saving rate had dropped to 17.6%. Germany was next with 13.8% (same as 1970) and the rates in France and Japan were close behind. In Canada, the savings rate had almost doubled to 11.5%. The UK and the USA had the lowest rates, 8.2% and 5.5% respectively.

By 2000 the savings rates had levelled out considerably across the seven countries. France and Japan led with 13.6%, followed by Germany, Italy and the UK at around 11%. Personal savings in North America dropped sharply, with the USA at 4% and Canada at a very low 1.9%.

The overall trend shows a reduction in savings over this thirty-year period.

(174 words)

Notes
- This essay shows a simple plan of organisation–the savings rate from highest to lowest in each of the 3 time periods.
- The challenge is to vary language use (say similar things in different ways) and to link the information smoothly.
- *Respectively* : a useful term for Task 1 essays. It means *'in that order'* eg *UK, US, 8.2% and 5.5% respectively.*
- Useful expressions for graph description: *most dramatic changes are evident, almost doubled, levelled out considerably, dropped sharply, the overall trend shows.*

WRITING

You should spend about 40 minutes on this task.

Prepare a written argument for a well-educated reader on the following topic:

> *Climate change is now an accepted threat to our planet, but there is not enough political action to control excessive consumerism and pollution. Do you agree?*

Write at least 250 words.

You should use your own ideas, knowledge and experience and support your arguments with examples and relevant evidence.

Step 1   Analyse the task   *Read carefully to understand all the details.*

What type of essay is it?	agree or disagree
What are the key words... ...related to the topic? ...related to the task?	climate change, political action, consumerism, pollution Do you agree?
Which terms need explaining?	climate change

Step 2   Generate Ideas   *Ask questions based on the key words.*

What kind of climate change?	global warming, rising sea levels, unpredictable weather patterns (storms, drought, floods)
...caused by?	industrial activity especially in the developed world
How is pollution connected to climate change?	Kyoto Agreement (intended to limit emissions) failed because of pressure from industry
How does consumerism relate to pollution/climate change?	modern lifestyle based on consumerism, cars, houses, having many things
How could political action be effective?	through schools pressure on industry
What are the problems?	traditional political parties support economic growth; environmental parties like Greens: good policies, little power

Step 3   Think it through   *Put your ideas in order before you start to write.*

Introduction	agree almost 100% (opinion based on evidence) define climate change
Paragraph topics	1 pollution eg... 2 consumerism eg... 3 political action eg... and problems eg...
Conclusion	plea for action to save planet; strong view, strongly expressed

Complete these activities based on the sample answer to build writing skills for Task 2 questions.

1   Compressing information

Academic writing tries to express information economically.
Find the expressions in the sample answer which use fewer words but mean the same as:

- The levels of the world's seas

  eg .....*sea levels*.....(2 words)

- The temperatures of the seas

  ....(2)

- The interests of those companies that have factories and offices in many countries

  ....(5)

- Policies about the environment which are responsible policies

  ....(3)

2   Use of present progressive

Find 2 examples of the present progressive tense, used in this essay to show the ongoing nature of the problems:

eg   .....*are recording*.....

- ....

- ....

3   Use of 'This'

What does 'this' refer to?

- (para 2) 'This is probably related to...' *This* refers to:.....................................

- (para 2) 'This keeps factories operating...' *This* refers to:.....................................

Answers: 1 sea temperatures / the interests of multinational corporations / responsible environmental policies
2 are rising / are increasing **3** unwillingness to change / good lifestyle

I agree entirely with the opinion in the title. There is increasing evidence that climate changes are not just random but are being accelerated by industrial activity, particularly in developed countries. Many nations are recording extreme weather conditions, such as the wettest year on record, or the hottest summer on record. Sea levels are rising and sea temperatures are increasing more rapidly than before.

The Kyoto Agreement in the 1990s tried to create international consensus to limit industrial emissions of gases but unfortunately some nations are unwilling to commit to real change. This is probably related to economic pressures from within the country and the interests of multinational corporations. In industrialised nations a good lifestyle means a high level of consumerism. This keeps factories operating and people employed but it also creates enormous pollution and waste.

To solve these serious problems requires political action in a number of directions. At the individual level, education programs in schools should be set up to reduce wasteful behaviour and to encourage respect for the planet. At the corporate level, businesses need to develop responsible environmental policies together with governments. They must be held legally accountable for their actions.

One major difficulty is that environmental parties like the Greens have little political power. Their policies are appropriate but they need support from the general public in order to increase pressure on the main parties and large corporations.

The time for action is definitely now. Each year of delays and ineffective policy will make it harder to restore the health of planet Earth.

(264 words)

Notes

- This essay asks your opinion, so it is appropriate to say: 'I agree entirely with...'
- The argument in each paragraph is structured around a topic sentence followed by examples to give evidence/support. A simple plan is to build each paragraph of the body around a key word/idea from the question. Write the topic sentence and develop the rest of the paragraph with examples and supporting ideas.
- To maintain relevance to the topic, arguments focus on climate change only, not on other environmental problems.

WRITING

You should spend about 20 minutes on this task.

The diagrams below show how chocolate is made and how the price of a chocolate bar is divided up among those involved in the process.
Write a report for a lecturer describing the information presented.

Write at least 150 words.

How chocolate is made

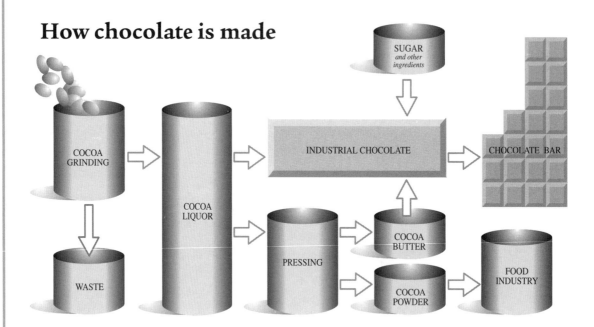

How the price of a chocolate bar is divided up

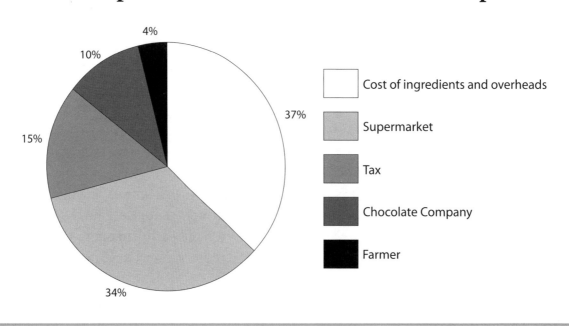

Analyse the task   *Look at the question, title and subtitle.*
Highlight key words.

Think it through

Description   *Put the 5 steps (A-E) for making chocolate in the correct order.*
(Process diagram)   *Write the sentences in full to develop Paragraph 1 structure.*

> The process of making chocolate begins with...
>
> **A** liquor/either/pressed/become/cocoa powder/sell/food industry
>
> **B** add/sugar etc/refine/produce/chocolate bar
>
> **C** or/pressed/become/cocoa butter
>
> **D** grind cocoa/produce/cocoa liquor/waste products
>
> **E** industrial chocolate/make from/cocoa liquor, cocoa butter

Description   *Ask questions to find the information you need.*
(Pie chart)   *Then use the gapped sample answer (part) as a writing guide.*

How to paraphrase the title as a topic sentence?

What is a logical sequence?
1 start with first step, also most significant information

2 contrast with remaining amounts

3 end with largest percentage

Conclusion
Interesting comment?

> How is the .... from the retail ....
> of a chocolate bar .... up?
>
> The pie chart indicates that the farmer who ....
> the .... receives only .... of
> the retail price.
>
> The ...., on the other hand, receives 34%.
> A rather small 10% .... to the chocolate
> company while 15% is taken by the .... in
> the form of taxes.
>
> The cost of .... and production, make up
> the largest proportion, 37% of the .... of a
> chocolate bar.
>
> It seems unfair that the .... , who do so
> .... work, get .... a small return for
> their efforts.

Complete these activities based on the sample answer to build writing skills for Task 1 questions.

1   Use of the passive

Find 6 verbs in the passive voice from the sample answer.

Note: 'becomes' does not have a passive form

eg   *is used*
....

....

....

2   Tricky little words

What little word comes immediately after these words from the sample answer.

Cocoa butter is used along   ....

Ingredients and production make   ....

How is the money divided   ....

10% goes   ....

3   Synonyms

From the sample answer find synonyms for:

to produce (paragraph 1)   ....

get (para 2)   ....

goes to (para 2)   ....

Answers: **1** can be sold / is combined / is refined / is divided up / is taken   **2** with / up / up / to
3 to make / receives / is taken by

The process of making chocolate begins with the grinding of the cocoa bean, to produce cocoa liquor and some waste products. The liquor is used in two ways. When pressed into powder it can be sold on to the food industry. Alternatively when pressed into cocoa butter it is used, along with the liquor to make industrial chocolate. This is combined with sugar and other ingredients and refined to produce chocolate bars.

How is the money from the retail price of a chocolate bar divided up? The pie chart indicates that the farmer, who produces the cocoa bean, receives only 4% of the retail price. The supermarket, on the other hand receives 34%. A rather small 10% goes to the chocolate company, while 15 % is taken by the government in the form of taxes. The cost of ingredients and production, make up the largest proportion, 37% of the price of a chocolate bar.

It seems unfair that the farmers, who do so much of the work, get such a small return for their efforts.

(178 words)

Notes

- Useful language for describing a process: *...begins with / ...either....or / ...which is then / ...in order to make / ...after that / ...further / ...finally*
- In this task there are two diagrams to describe. The obvious way to organise the essay is to write one short paragraph on each diagram. With 5 minutes planning time that leaves 7 minutes (approximately 75 words) per paragraph. Keep it simple.
- Impersonal language is generally used in academic writing and Task 1s. The following is an exception: *'From the pie chart we can see...'*
- A useful and concise introduction is the question in Paragraph 2: *'How is the money..... divided up?'*
- For emphasis the highest percentage of cost is put last as a separate sentence.
- A comment/observation can be an effective conclusion, if you are under the minimum word length.

WRITING

You should spend about 40 minutes on this task.

Prepare a written argument for a well-educated reader on the following topic:

> *Many people keep dogs and cats as companions. Discuss the advantages and disadvantages of pet ownership for the animals involved and for the community as a whole.*

Write at least 250 words.

You should use your own ideas, knowledge and experience and support your arguments with examples and relevant evidence.

Step 1 Analyse the task
Read carefully to understand all the details.

What type of essay is it?	two sides of an argument
What are the key words...	
...related to the topic?	dogs/cats/pet ownership/community
...related to the task?	advantages and disadvantages

Step 2 Generate Ideas
Ask questions based on the key words.

Brainstorm 'pet ownership'

	What are the advantages?	What are the disadvantages?
For the animals?	• loved, cared for, well-fed	• lack of freedom and natural activity: kept indoors at night and belled (cats), on lead, muzzled (dogs)

For the community?	• pet owners healthier and happier
	• service: guide and guard dogs
		• not always well-treated and respected
		• more regulations:
		  to protect native animals from cats
		  to control dogs
		• cost of abandoned pets

Step 3 Think it through
Put your ideas in order before you start to write.

Introduction	paraphrase task statement to restate both sides of issue

Paragraph topics	1 advantages of pets: for animals
	  for owners
	  for community
	2 disadvantages: for pets
	  for community

Conclusion	complex relationship restate main idea in a new way

1 Use of Passives

Put the passive form of these verbs to complete these phrases using the sample answer:

feed care for love give restrict keep impose require abandon

- …pets are **f**................. and **c**................. and **l**.................
- It is easy to see how much attention is ....
- The freedoms are increasingly ....
- Dogs must be .... on leads
- These restrictions have been ....
- …pet owners are .... to clean up…
- …dogs and cats that have been .... by owners

2 Connecting expressions

Find the missing connecting expressions indicated for each paragraph. (NOT 'and')

(para 1) / ....

(para 2) / *in return* / *not only, but* / .... /

(para 3) / .... / *no longer, but* / .... / ....

(para 4) .... / ....

3 Compressing language

Find the expression in the sample answer for:

- the owning of pets .... *(2 words)*

- the part of the supermarket where pet products are

  sold .... (5)

- owners who do not take responsibility .... (2)

Answers: 1 fed, cared for, loved, given, restricted, kept, imposed, required, abandoned **2** (para 1) but, (para 2) thus, (para 3) however / in addition / also, (para 4) so / still **3** pet ownership / the pet section of supermarkets / irresponsible owners

Dogs and cats can be wonderful companions but there are also a number of problems associated with pet ownership, both for the animals and for the community.

In the best situations pets are fed, cared for and loved as part of a family. It is easy to see how much attention is given to pets, by the range of products available in the pet section of supermarkets. In return, cats and dogs contribute to the well being of the community in many ways. Dogs are useful for protection and serve as guides for the disabled. People with pets are not only happier and healthier, but may even live longer. Thus the animals benefit individuals and the community as well.

There are, however, also negative aspects for the pets and for the community. The freedoms of both dogs and cats are increasingly restricted. In Australia there is community pressure to force owners to keep cats inside at night to protect native birds and animals. Dogs can no longer run free in parks and at the beach but must be kept on leads. These restrictions have been imposed by the community to protect the public. In addition pet owners are required to clean up after their dogs. Parks and beaches often provide plastic bags for this purpose. The community also has to pick up the costs of dogs and cats that have been abandoned by irresponsible owners.

So the relationship between pets and the community is a complex one. More and more the community is intervening to force pet owners to restrict the activities and freedom of their pets. Still, responsible owners, prepared to give adequate time and attention to their cats and dogs, can give them a good and happy life.

(290 words)

Notes

- Task words: *'Many people keep dogs and cats...'* Paraphrase: *'Dogs and cats can be wonderful companions.'*
- This essay is organised into 2 paragraphs: advantages/disadvantages. Each paragraph includes 2 aspects – for the pet, for the community. Each point has an example to support it.
- The argument balances positives and negatives and the conclusion reflects both sides.

WRITING | TEST 4 | TASK 1

You should spend about 20 minutes on this task.

> *The two graphs below show the percentage of smokers and the consumption of alcohol in litres in selected countries, for the period 1960 – 2000.*
> *Write a report for a lecturer describing the information in the graphs.*

Write at least 150 words.

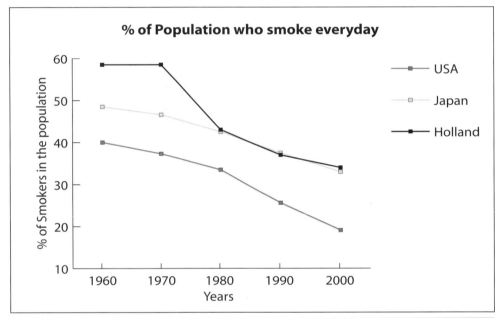

% of Population who smoke everyday

Legend: USA, Japan, Holland

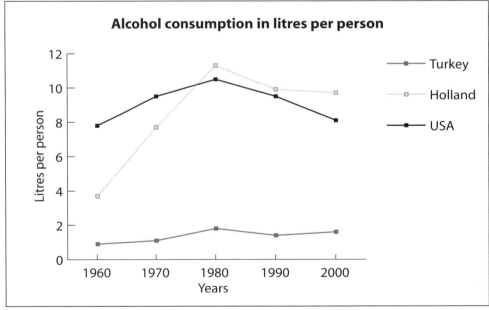

Alcohol consumption in litres per person

Legend: Turkey, Holland, USA

Analyse the task   *Look at the question, title and subtitle.*
Highlight key words.

Think it through   *Ask questions to find the information you need.*
Then use the gapped sample answer as a guide.

Introduction

> The two .... graphs show trends .... smoking and alcohol consumption .... 1960 for several ....

Description (Graph 1)

What is the general trend?

Which year to start with and what order?

What is the trend through 1980 and 2000 for each country?

> In terms .... smoking patterns, the general .... in the USA, ... and Holland is downwards. .... had the highest percentage of smokers in .... at nearly 60%, ... by Japan at about 47% and the USA at .... 40%. Holland experienced the .... dramatic decrease, falling .... about 43% in 1980 and then declined at the same .... rate as .... until 2000. USA's .... fell to below 20% by ....

Description (Graph 2)

How to signal the change of topic and make a general comment?

What is the best order to put the information in?

Which countries have a similar trend?

Which country has a different pattern?

> Turning .... alcohol consumption, the story .... different.
>
> The number of .... per capita consumed in Holland and the .... increased sharply between 1960 and .... from around 4 litres per .... in Holland to about .... in 1980 and from nearly 8 litres to .... than 10 in the USA in 1980. Thereafter .... countries' consumption declined .... to around 8 litres .... the USA in 2000 and 10 in Holland.
> The .... in Turkey was rather different. Turkey's .... remained low, rising only .... from 1 litre to about 1.5 litres per person between 1960 and 2000.

Conclusion

How to explain these trends?

Complete these activities based on the sample answer to build writing skills for Task 1 questions.

1 Qualifiers

Write the adverb or adjective from the text to complete the notes:

Holland

1960 – 80 .... decrease in smoking

1960 - 80, alcohol drinking increased .... Post 1980 declined ....

Turkey

1960 - 2000 alcohol consumption rose ....

2 Synonyms - odd one out

Which word in each group is not a synonym of the others?

- approximately   about   until   around
- a little below   slightly less than   well under
- much more than   somewhat more than   a lot more than   well above
- declined   dropped   fell   stabilised   decreased   went down
- rose   went from   went up   increased

3 Economical sentences

Using the sample answer, try to write these sentences in a more economical way.

- The number of litres per capita which were consumed in Holland and the USA increased sharply...   *(save 2 words)*

- Turkey's consumption remained low. Its consumption rose only slightly.... between 1960 and 2000.   *(save 2 words)*

- Holland experienced the most dramatic decrease. Holland's percentage fell to about 43% in 1980...   *(save 2 words)*

Answers: **1** dramatic / sharply / steadily / slightly **2** until / well under / somewhat more than / stabilised / went from **3** consumed (which were consumed) /, rising (its consumption rose) /, falling (Holland's percentage fell)

The two line graphs show trends in smoking and alcohol consumption since 1960 for several countries.

In terms of smoking patterns, the general trend in the USA, Japan and Holland is downwards. Holland had the highest percentage of smokers in 1960 at nearly 60%, followed by Japan at about 47% and the USA at around 40%. Holland experienced the most dramatic decrease, falling to about 43% in 1980 and then declined at the same steady rate as Japan until 2000. USA's level fell to below 20% by 2000.

Turning to alcohol consumption, the story is different. The number of litres per capita consumed in Holland and the USA increased sharply between 1960 and 1980 from around 4 litres per person in Holland to about 11 in 1980 and from nearly 8 litres to more than 10 in the USA. Thereafter both countries' consumption declined steadily to around 8 litres in the USA in 2000 and 10 in Holland. The pattern in Turkey was rather different. Turkey's consumption remained low, rising only slightly from 1 to about 1.5 litres per person between 1960 and 2000.

(186 words)

Notes
- Graph vocabulary: *trends / downwards / highest percentage / followed by dramatic decrease / falling to / steady decline*
- Topic sentences in each paragraph use economical signal expressions: *'In terms of' / 'Turning to'*...
- *'Per capita'* is a useful synonym for *'per person'.*

WRITING

You should spend about 40 minutes on this task.

Prepare a written argument for a well-educated reader on the following topic:

> *We live today in an electronic information age. It is easier to be connected by technology yet many people seem no closer to feeling happy in their lives. Discuss.*

Write at least 250 words.

You should use your own ideas, knowledge and experience and support your arguments with examples and relevant evidence.

Step 1 Analyse the task

Read carefully to understand all the details.

What type of essay is it?

What are the key words...
    ...related to the topic?

    ...related to the task?
Which terms need explaining?

---

two sides of an argument

electronic information age, happy lives

discuss
happy / connected

Step 2 Generate Ideas

Ask questions based on the key words.

What are the advantages of the electronic age?

- email / internet / chatrooms (easy quick cheap contact)
- contact with family, friends (old / new)
- technology can overcome isolation eg Finland

Are we happier?

isolated at computer (only on-line friends?)

Evidence of lack of happiness?

rates of depression / suicide / divorce / stress

Step 3 Think it through

Put your ideas in order before you start to write.

Introduction

What is happiness? How is it related to being connected?

Paragraph topics

1 advantages of technology (on the one hand)

2 disadvantages (on the other hand)

Conclusion

summarise / indicate your opinion

Complete these activities based on the sample answer to build writing skills for Task 2 questions.

1 Synonyms

Which of the expressions in each group is not a synonym of the others?

- to communicate / to contact / to be connected / to overcome / to stay in touch
- rates / cases / levels
- for example / via / like / such as

2 Compressing information

Which shorter expressions in the sample answer mean the same as:

- the rate at which people are getting divorced *(Find 2 words)*
- the amounts of stress that are being experienced (2)
- websites on the internet where people can make dates with one another (3)
- the age in which there is a lot of information available (2)
- a call on the telephone (2)
- the levels at which people use the internet (4)

3 Could this be used instead?

*Could the expression on the right directly replace the expression in the sample answer? Answer **Yes or No**.*

Expressions in the sample answer		Could this be used instead?	
In this way... (para 2)		After this,...	(Y / N)
For example (para 2)		For instance...	(Y / N)
Similarly... (para 2)		In a similar way...	(Y / N)
Even so... (para 4)		Nevertheless...	(Y / N)
...therefore... (para 4)		...so...	(Y / N)

Answers 1 overcome / case / via **2** divorce rate / stress levels / internet dating sites/ information age / telephone call / rates of internet use **3** N / Y / Y / Y / N

The electronic information age that we live in today, certainly makes communicating very quick and easy. It is simple for many people to contact dozens of others every day via computer or phone, but does this make them feel happier? Happiness is difficult to define, but in addition to basic needs like food, shelter or peace, it depends on such things as good health, a loving family and friends, and a satisfying occupation - either job, study or pastime. Whether modern communication has increased people's feelings of happiness is, however, debatable.

There are many advantages to being connected electronically. For the price of a local phone call we can stay in touch via email with family or friends around the world. In this way isolation by distance or climate can be overcome. For example, Finland with its long winter has one of the highest rates of internet use. Information that would only be available to a small number of people without the use of computers is now at our fingertips. Similarly thousands of people use chatrooms and internet dating sites every day.

On the other hand it seems to be the case that depression and suicide rates are high and the divorce rate is increasing. Employees complain of longer working hours and increased stress levels. There is concern that people are in fact becoming more isolated, only communicating on-line. On this evidence they seem unhappier today.

Happiness is hard to measure, as it is subjective and depends on the particular situation. Perhaps there is more awareness of current problems because so much information is available through technology and the media. Even so, it would seem that the quality of our relationships and therefore our level of happiness is unrelated to modern technology, which is, after all, only a tool.

(299 words)

Notes
- The 'thesis statement' (last sentence of the introduction) tells the reader that the body of the essay will give arguments both for and against '........is debatable.'
- Useful expressions for a discussion essay:
  'there is concern that'... means that some people are worried about the situation...
  'perhaps'... shows that the writer is considering possible reasons for these problems
  'it would seem that'... indicates something is probable rather than 100% certain.

WRITING | TEST 5 TASK 1

You should spend about 20 minutes on this task.

The table below shows the results of an airline survey in 2002 of economy class business travellers. The numbers indicate how many male or female passengers in each age group rated a particular feature as their most important in-flight consideration.
Write a report for a lecturer describing the information in the table.

Write at least 150 words.

IN-FLIGHT FEATURE RANKED FIRST	Females		Males	
	Age 25-45	45+	25-45	45+
SEAT / LEG ROOM	30	35	39	46
MEALS / DRINKS	26	31	20	24
ATTENDANT SERVICE	34	30	27	26
MOVIES / IN-FLIGHT ENTERTAINMENT	10	4	14	4
TOTALS INTERVIEWED	**100**	**100**	**100**	**100**

Analyse the task

Look at the question, title and subtitle.
Highlight key words.

Think it through

Ask questions to find the information you need.
Then use the gapped sample answer as a guide.

Introduction

What does the table show?

The table .... in-flight preferences of 400 regular male and .... , economy class travellers in .... age groups, based on an airline .... in 2002.

Description

What were the men's in-flight preferences?
(from highest to lowest)

Specifically, 39 of the 100 men .... 25-45 rated seat/leg room as the most important .... , rising to 46 of the older men. Service was next .... 27 of the 25-45 male group and 26 of .... 45+ group rating that .... After that at 20 and 24 respectively comes meals/drinks. Last is entertainment, chosen by only 14 of the younger and 4 of the .... males.

What were the women's preferences?
(from lowest to highest)

.... to the female groups, ... is clear that entertainment is .... of low importance with .... 10 of the younger and 4 .... the older age group .... it first. Drinks and meals .... rated number one by 26 .... women and 31 of the .... 45s. Service and seat/leg room .... the most important in-flight .... for women, with 34 younger and .... older women choosing the former .... 30 and 35 chose the ....

Conclusion

What observation or comment can be made?

The high .... of physical comfort for .... air travellers seems undeniable.

Complete these activities based on the sample answer to develop writing skills for Task 1 questions.

1   Prepositions

Write the appropriate preposition for each expression from the sample answer.

Based .... / .... low importance / rising .... / Turning .... / chosen .... /

high priority .... / preferences of travellers .... two age groups

2   Comparison language

Complete the sentences:

- Older men rate .... as more important than older women do.

- Younger women rate .... and service more highly than older women do.

- The most important in-flight factor is ....

- The least important consideration is ....

- The second most important feature for men is ....

- .... seem about as important as service for 45+ women.

3   Synonyms

Find synonyms in the sample answer for these expressions:

- ...rated number one...   ....

- Last is...   ....

- younger men   ....

- 45+ males   ....

- 25 – 45 year old females   ....

Answers: 1 on / of / to / to / by / of / in **2** seat & leg room / entertainment / seat & leg room / entertainment / service / meals & drinks **3** placed first, the high priority / of low importance / 25- 45 male group / older men / younger women

The table indicates in-flight preferences of 400 regular male and female economy class travellers in two age groups, based on an airline survey in 2002.

Specifically 39 of the 100 men aged 25-45 rated seat/leg room as the most important feature, rising to 46 of the older men. Service was next with 27 of the 25-45 male group and 26 of the 45+ group rating that first. After that, at 20 and 24 respectively comes meals/drinks. Last is entertainment, chosen by only 14 of the younger and 4 of the 45+ males.

Turning to the female groups, it is clear that entertainment is also of low importance with only 10 of the younger and 4 of the older age group placing it first. Drinks and meals are rated number one by 26 younger women and 31 of the over 45s. Service and seat/leg room are the most important in-flight features for women, with 34 younger and 30 older women choosing the former, while 30 and 35 chose the latter.

The high priority of physical comfort for frequent air travellers seems undeniable.

(178 words)

Notes

- The introduction summarises the task title economically and the writer has managed to include all of the data in the answer by using a condensed style.
- Paragraph 1 ends with 'entertainment' so to link into paragraph 2, entertainment is addressed first, then the leading preferences. For consistency, the younger age group is always mentioned first.
- The writer uses 'ellipsis' (ie leaving out words without losing meaning) to save words, as in '...the younger men (who were) interviewed'; ' Last is entertainment, (which was) chosen by...'
- You can avoid clumsy repetition by using synonyms. For example, the writer avoids repeating 'in the 25-45 year old group' by using the simpler expression 'in the younger group'; or by using 'the over 45s' instead of 'the 45+ age group'.
Synonyms also give variety, avoiding a boring style of report:
most important feature / rated number one / placing it first / rating that first.

WRITING

You should spend about 40 minutes on this task.

Prepare a written argument for a well-educated reader on the following topic:

> *Most developed countries spend a large proportion of their health budgets on expensive medical technology and procedures. This money should be spent instead on health education to keep people well. To what extent do you agree or disagree with this opinion?*

Write at least 250 words.

You should use your own ideas, knowledge and experience and support your arguments with examples and relevant evidence.

Step 1 Analyse the task

Read carefully to understand all the details.

What type of essay is it?

> two sides of an argument

What are the key words...
>   ...related to the topic?

> expensive medical technology / procedures
> health education

>   ...related to the task?

> to what extent / agree disagree

Step 2 Generate Ideas

Ask questions based on the key words.

What kind of...
>   ...technology? (give examples)
>   ...procedures? (give examples)

> high-tech MRI scanners
> organ transplants / IVF

What is health education?

> learning how to stay well
> eg lifestyle changes, diet, exercise

Step 3 Think it through

Put your ideas in order before you start to write.

Introduction
(turn statement into questions)

> Why is the health budget spent this way?
> Why spend money on health education?

Paragraph topics

> 1 advantages of spending on health education
>   (on the one hand)

> 2 advantages of high tech hospital treatment
>   (on the other hand)

Conclusion

> Summarise and indicate opinion

Complete these activities based on the sample answer to build writing skills for Task 2 questions.

1 Compressing information

Which shorter expressions in the text mean the same as these?

- the amount of money planned for use on health *(Find 2 words)*

- problems connected with people's health (2)

- care which is given by nurses (2)

- sicknesses that are caused by the way people live (2)

- the transferring of a body part from one person into the body of another (2)

2 Word families

In the sample answer find 8 expressions connected to each of the following topics:

  (a) health
  (b) finance

3 Word groups - What's the next word?

Match the word(s) on the left from the sample essay with one on the right that follows it.

straightforward	world
it is questionable	term
the best treatment	whether
the long	issue
developed	possible

Answers: 1 health budget / health problems / nursing care / lifestyle diseases / organ transplants **2a** (examples) unwell, ill health, medical, doctor, sick, treatment, surgery, hospitalisation, diseases **2b** savings, budget, expensive, health dollar, spend, afford, costly, money **3** straightforward issue / questionable whether / treatment possible / the long term / developed world

Almost daily there are reports of new advances in medicine. In the developed world certainly, the prognosis for many medical problems is more optimistic today than ten years ago and continues to improve. But these developments in health care are very expensive, and it is questionable whether countries can afford to continue to increase spending on health. Many believe that it would be better to spend more preventing people from becoming unwell in the first place, and reduce the amount spent on curing ill health.

As many modern diseases are a consequence of our lifestyles, one way of making savings to the health budget would be to educate people about how to prevent expensive health problems such as diabetes or heart disease. Most medical doctors today do not have the time to (nor are they paid to) teach patients how to make these changes to their lifestyle through diet or exercise.

It is understandable that when people are sick they want the best medical treatment possible, with access to the latest diagnostic equipment, expensive MRI scanners, for example. If the problem is life threatening then we demand complex operations such as open-heart surgery or organ transplants. Such procedures usually require intensive nursing care and lengthy periods of hospitalisation, which are costly.

Thus it can be seen that this is not a straightforward issue and depends to some extent on one's situation. While the 'health dollar' is limited, however, it would seem rational to direct more resources towards the prevention of ill health. In this way fewer people would become ill from these preventable lifestyle diseases. In the long term this should save the country money and increase the well-being of the population.

(290 words)

Notes

- The wording of the question is decisive eg 'should be spent' whereas the wording of the answer is qualified eg *'Many believe it would be preferable'*, *'it would seem rational'*, *'where larger numbers may benefit'*
- In this essay, statements are regularly followed by examples which help to explain, clarify and develop the idea.

  'preventable lifestyle diseases' examples given are *diabetes, heart disease*

  'lifestyle changes' – *diet, exercise*

  'expensive diagnostic equipment' – *MRI scanners*

  'expensive operations' – *open-heart surgery, organ transplants*
- Use of linking words: *similarly / such* procedures / *thus* it can be seen / *however* / *In this way*

You should spend about 20 minutes on this task.

> *The graph and table show the number of fishers in millions for different regions between 1970, 1980 and 2000, and the world's top ten exporters of fish in 2000.*
> *Write a report for a lecturer describing the information shown.*

Write at least 150 words.

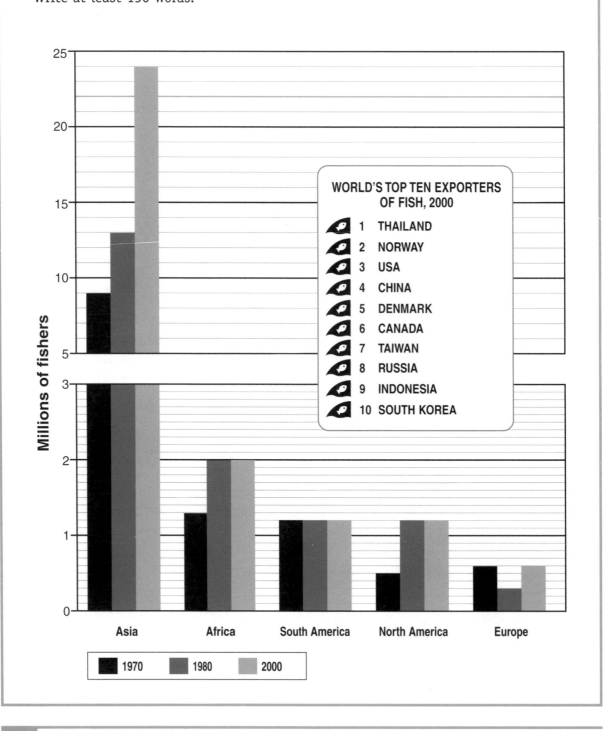

Analyse the task

Look at the question, title and subtitle.
Highlight key words. Identify the main trends.

Think it through

Ask questions to find the information you need.
Then use the gapped sample answer as a guide.

Introduction

What are the most significant statistics?

The graph and table .... that Asia is the region of the world .... the largest .... of fishers in 1970, 1980 and 2000, at 9 million, 13 million and 24 million .... No other region has seen such .... increases in numbers.

Description of graph

What about remaining regions? (in descending order of importance describe both the numbers of fishers and the trends)

Africa's fishers .... 1.3 million in 1970, and .... in both 1980 and 2000. South America had steady numbers of fishers, 1.2 million, ... the period. In North America .... were 0.5 million fishers in 1970 and the numbers increased to .... 1.2 million in 1980, a number that remained .... in 2000. Europe had the fewest fishers with 0.6 million in 1970 .... to 0.3 million in 1980 and .... to 0.6 million in 2000.

Description of table

How to signal transition to new topic/paragraph and identify most significant data?
What is the logical way to group remaining countries?

.... to the table of exporters, Thailand is the world's .... exporter of fish, but European and North American countries are also ....
Norway and Denmark take second and fifth places .... , while the USA is the third .... exporter and Canada ranks .... China and Taiwan .... fourth and seventh places while Russia, ... and South Korea complete the table in eighth, ninth and tenth ....

Conclusion

How to explain this trend?

To .... , there are more fishers in Asia .... in the rest of the world combined.

Complete these activities based on the sample answer to develop writing skills for Task 1 questions.

1 Synonyms

Choose a synonym to match each expression from the sample answer.

implies / spectacular / show / reducing / significant / conclude / stayed the same

In the sample answer	Synonym
indicate	....
dramatic	....
remained unchanged	....
contracting	....
prominent	....
summarise	....
suggests	....

2 Listing positions in a table

Match the country from the table with the appropriate expression.

the second largest, the biggest, in fifth position, the third largest, the lowest ranked, in fourth spot

Country	
Denmark	....
Thailand	....
USA	....
South Korea	....
Norway	....
China	....

3 Prepositions

What preposition goes with each expression in the sample answer?

- dramatic increases .... numbers...
- increasing .... about 1.2 million...
- returning .... 0.6 million...
- Turning .... the table of exporters...
- .... eighth, ninth and tenth spots.
- .... summarise...

Answers: 1 indicate – show / dramatic – spectacular / remained unchanged - stayed the same / contracting – reducing / prominent – significant / summarise - conclude / suggests - implies **2** Denmark - in fifth position, Thailand - the biggest, USA- the third largest, South Korea - the lowest ranked, Norway - the second largest, China - in fourth spot, **3** in / to / to / to / in / To

The graph and table indicate that Asia is the region of the world with the largest numbers of fishers in 1970, 1980 and 2000, at 9, 13 and 24 million respectively. No other region has seen such dramatic increases in numbers. Africa's fishers numbered 1.3 million in 1970, and 2 million in both 1980 and 2000. South America had steady numbers of fishers, 1.2 million, throughout the period. In North America there were 0.5 million fishers in 1970 increasing to about 1.2 million in 1980, a number that remained unchanged in 2000. Europe had the fewest fishers with 0.6 million in 1970 contracting to 0.3 million in 1980 and returning to 0.6 million in 2000.

Turning to the table of exporters, Thailand is the world's top exporter of fish, but European and North American countries are also prominent. Norway and Denmark take second and fifth places respectively, while the USA is the third largest exporter and Canada ranks sixth. China and Taiwan occupy fourth and seventh places while Russia, Indonesia and South Korea complete the table in eighth, ninth and tenth spots.

To summarise, there are more fishers in Asia than in the rest of the world combined.

(198 words)

Notes
- 'Fishers' has replaced 'fishermen' as a gender-neutral term to include women who work in the industry and catch fish for a living.
- 'Turning to' indicates transition to a new paragraph and a new topic – from the graph to the table.
- In the second paragraph, European countries are grouped together, then North American to give variety and to follow the topic sentence order.
- Use variety to avoid repetition: *top exporter / take second place / is the third largest exporter / occupy fourth place / ranks sixth / in eighth... spots.*

You should spend about 40 minutes on this task.

Prepare a written argument for a well-educated reader on the following topic:

> *Because of the pressure of new subjects such as business studies, many schools have dropped sport or physical education (PE) from the curriculum. How important is sport or PE in a young person's education?*

Write at least 250 words.

You should use your own ideas, knowledge and experience and support your arguments with examples and relevant evidence.

Step 1   Analyse the task

Read carefully to understand all the details.

What type of essay is it?	evaluate an argument
What are the key words... ...related to the topic?	sport / physical education
...related to the task?	How important ...

Step 2   Generate Ideas

Ask questions based on the key words.

Why is sport/ physical education being replaced on the school curriculum?	low priority compared to employment–related subjects
What is the value of PE in school?	break from mental activity, better concentration on school work, exercise, fitness, learn new sports
How important is it?	as important as any subject 'fitness for life'

Step 3   Think it through

Put your ideas in order before you start to write.

Introduction	Question asks 'How important?' Answer: 'of vital importance'

Paragraph topics	1 problem of academic demands and time pressure
	    PE improves concentration and performance
	
	2 problem of obesity, sedentary lifestyle of many students
	    PE offers exercise, new activities, fitness for life

Conclusion	summarise and re-state opinion

Complete these activities based on the sample answer to build writing skills for Task 2 questions.

1 Connecting expressions

Could the expression in brackets ( ) be used instead of these connecting expressions in the sample answer without making other changes? **Yes or No?**

- It is true that (Even though) (para 1)   Y / N
- As a result (Nevertheless) (1)   Y / N
- While (Whereas) (1)   Y / N
- so that (since) (2)   Y / N
- In addition (As well) (3)   Y / N
- In conclusion (To summarise) (4)   Y / N
- The result will be (As a consequence) (4)   Y / N

2 Synonyms

Which of the expressions in each group is not a synonym of the others?

- program   curriculum   class
- unfortunate   unavoidable   inevitable
- sedentary   uncooperative   inactive
- overweight   lazy   obese   fat

3 Scrambled word groups

Rewrite these scrambled word groups from the sample answer.

- true is that it... (para 1)   ....
- education is ground physical losing... (1)   ....
- shift inevitable see as this many... (1)   ....
- argue I that would... (1)   ....
- is concern growing a there ... (3)   ....
- sport in enjoy participating ... (4)   ....

Answers: 1 N / N / Y / N / Y / Y / N **2** class / unfortunate / uncooperative / lazy **3** see sample answer

It is true that there is increasing pressure on schools today to prepare their students for work in the twenty-first century. As a result, physical education is losing ground on the school curriculum to employment-related subjects like business. While many see this shift as inevitable, I would argue that physical education is a vital part of the school program and should be maintained. Sport and PE add variety to the curriculum, broaden the students' experience and teach essential life skills.

Within the school day, students need physical activity to balance the long hours spent sitting at desks. PE provides a break from the mental focus of academic subjects. A good PE program should include a variety of sports plus non-competitive activities like dance and aerobics so that students can experience exercise as both challenging and fun.

There is a growing concern among parents and educators about obesity in children. Many young people have a sedentary lifestyle that revolves around TV, computers and being driven in cars. Physical education ensures that all students get some form of regular exercise during the school day. In addition they learn about the importance of looking after their bodies.

In conclusion, physical education programs in schools are not only worth maintaining, they should be developed. The result will be students who are happier, healthier and more productive in class. They will grow into adults who value fitness and enjoy participating in sport. These are lessons for a lifetime, as important as any subject on the school curriculum.

(252 words)

Notes

- The 'thesis statement' acknowledges the counter argument: '... *many see this shift as inevitable*. It also indicates the position of the writer '*I would argue that*' and answers the question 'How important?' '...*physical education is a vital part of the curriculum and should be maintained.*'
- Both paragraphs of the body of the essay begin by stating a problem and showing how physical education helps to solve that problem, thereby demonstrating its value.
- The conclusion re-states the writer's opinion and reinforces the evaluation, answering the question '*How important?*'
- The essay is concise – just over the minimum number of words, but fulfills the task requirements.

UNIT 4 SPEAKING

WHAT'S AHEAD...
IN THE SPEAKING UNIT

- The IELTS Speaking Test

- *Fast Track Speaking*

- Instructions for Test Practice

- Speaking Test 1 (CD1)

    Questions and activities

- Speaking Test 2 (CD2)

    Questions and activities

- More Practice Questions

THE IELTS SPEAKING TEST

WHAT SHOULD I KNOW ABOUT IT?

Structure of the new test

The IELTS Speaking Test was revised in 2001. The format was changed and the way instructions and questions are given was standardised.

Your Speaking Test is with one interviewer. This interviewer also assesses your performance.

The test takes from 11-14 minutes and has THREE parts.

4-5 minutes

Your name and ID are checked and then you answer set questions on 3 familiar topics.

In more detail...

The interviewer will introduce her/himself and check your name, country and ID (passport or student card). A cassette recorder will be switched on to record your interview in case it needs to be checked. The test begins with the interviewer asking set questions on three topics. There are about 4 questions per topic, which means an average of 25 seconds per question. Try to say more than 'yes' or 'no' by extending your answers a little.

3-4 minutes

You are given a topic, which you have to talk about for 1-2 minutes. You have 1 minute to plan your talk. The interviewer asks 1 or 2 follow-up questions.

In more detail...

The interviewer gives you a card with your topic on it. Be sure to read the 3 or 4 details on the card carefully and answer all of them in your talk. If you take longer than two minutes, the interviewer will stop you, and then will ask one or two questions to finish off this part. Just answer them briefly.

Part 3

4-5 minutes

You have a discussion with the interviewer about issues related to the topic of the talk in Part 2.

In more detail...

The questions in Part 3 are more challenging but the interaction is more natural. The interviewer will respond to what you say but is testing your ability to use more complex language and express your ideas clearly and appropriately. When the test comes to an end, the interviewer is not permitted to discuss your performance or your score, so don't ask.

WHAT IS THE EXAMINER LOOKING FOR?

Assessment Criteria	In other words...
Fluency and coherence	Can you speak without pausing or hesitating? Can you use idiomatic expressions and develop your ideas using good connecting language?
Vocabulary	Can you use a good range of appropriate expressions to keep talking about and extending different topics easily?
Grammatical range and accuracy	What range of grammar and verb forms can you use flexibly, appropriately and accurately?
Pronunciation	How clearly can you be understood and how effectively can you use English stress and intonation?

Amira's tip:

While I was waiting outside the room, I had a snack and a drink to keep my energy up. I tried to relax by breathing slowly and doing some stretches. My interview was a little late. We had been told not to knock on the door so I just stayed nearby until I was called into the room by the examiner.

Natalya's tip:

'I'm quite shy so I got my identification ready to show the assessor before the test started and when I gave it to her I made eye contact and smiled. She smiled back so I felt more relaxed when I started to answer the questions.'

EXAMINERS' SUGGESTIONS

Here are some typical problems and questions that come up when students prepare for the Speaking Test, along with suggestions for improvement.

What happens if...?	Suggestions
... I don't understand a question.	Don't remain silent. Ask the interviewer politely to repeat the question. It's fine to say, 'Sorry?' or 'Pardon?' or 'Could you repeat the question, please?' These are good speaking strategies.
... I don't understand even after the question has been repeated.	You can just say 'I'm sorry, I still don't understand'. The interviewer will move on to another question.
... I understand the question but don't know how to answer.	Don't be worried that there is a correct answer to a question. The interviewer is just asking your opinion and basically wants to hear you speak. You can talk about the situation in your country or your personal experience.
... I have prepared some answers in advance and memorised them.	It will be obvious to the interviewer if you have learned answers by memory and you will lose marks. Practise lots but don't memorise. It is important to interact naturally and to be spontaneous.
...I can't think of enough to say to keep talking in Part 2.	Practise recording yourself making little speeches. Start with easy, familiar topics and a short time limit. Gradually increase your time and choose topics that are more difficult.

Hiroshi's tip:

'My problem was that I spoke slowly and had too many pauses. So, to practise, I recorded my answer to one question again and again until I could do it without pausing. I also practised several times with a clock, trying to give the same answer in fewer seconds. It worked. I got a 7 for Speaking!'

FAST TRACK SPEAKING

INSTRUCTIONS FOR TEST PRACTICE

There are TWO Sample Speaking Tests **2**

Speaking Test 1 (Zsuzso)

Before you listen, **look at the interview questions.** (p186)
Listen to the **whole interview first.**
> **OR**

Listen and do the activities **one part at a time.** (pp187-189)

Next...

Go back to the interview questions for Test 1.

Record **your** answers.

If possible, get a friend to ask you the questions
and record the whole interview.

Speaking Test 2 (Wen)

Follow the same steps.

Want more practice?

Use the additional practice questions on page 194.

Set questions

Topic 1: FAMILY

Do you come from a large or a small family?
Do all your family live in the same town or city?
How often do you see your brothers and sisters?
Do you have a lot in common with them?

Topic 2: FRIENDS

Do you have lots of friends or just a few special friends?
Can you say something about one or two of them?
What kinds of things do you and your friends like to do together?
Are you a person who enjoys spending time alone?

Topic 3: TRAVEL

Which other countries have you visited?
Which other countries are you interested in visiting? Why?
What are some of the things you don't like about travelling?

 Short talk

TOPIC CARD

Describe a favourite shop or store.
You should say:
> where it is and what it looks like
> what it sells
> what you like to buy there
and say why you like the shop so much.

 Discussion questions related to Shopping

What do you think of shopping on the Internet?
How do you think the use of the Internet will affect shopping in the future?
Why do you think that shopping has become such a popular activity for young people these days?
In what ways are your parents' shopping habits different from yours?
Can you give some examples of differences?
Do you think in wealthy countries people buy too many things they don't need?
Is that the case in your home country?